Johann Sebastian Bach

Six Suites for Cello solo BMV 1007-1012

Edited with annotations and remarks by

UZI WIESEL

for Arnan

Johann Sebastian Bach
Oil Painting by Hausmann 1746

Content

Köthen Mirror Hall i

Köthen Palace ii

Anna Magdalena 1730 Manuscript iii

Johann Peter Kellner 1726 Manuscript iv

German Copy Manuscript v

Austrian/German Copy Manuscript vi

First page of Lute Suite vii

Playing Bach 1

Argument 2

Introduction 3

Suite I 21

Suite II 32

Suite III 44

Suite IV 61

Suite V Scordatura 75

Suite V Normal Tuning 88

Suite V Normal Tuning after Lute MS 102

Suite VI 114

The Mirror Hall in Köthen Castle, Residence of Prince Leopold of Anhalt - Köthen, where J.S.Bach performed frequently during his time in Köthen (1717 – 1723).

Prince Leopold of Anhalt-Köthen

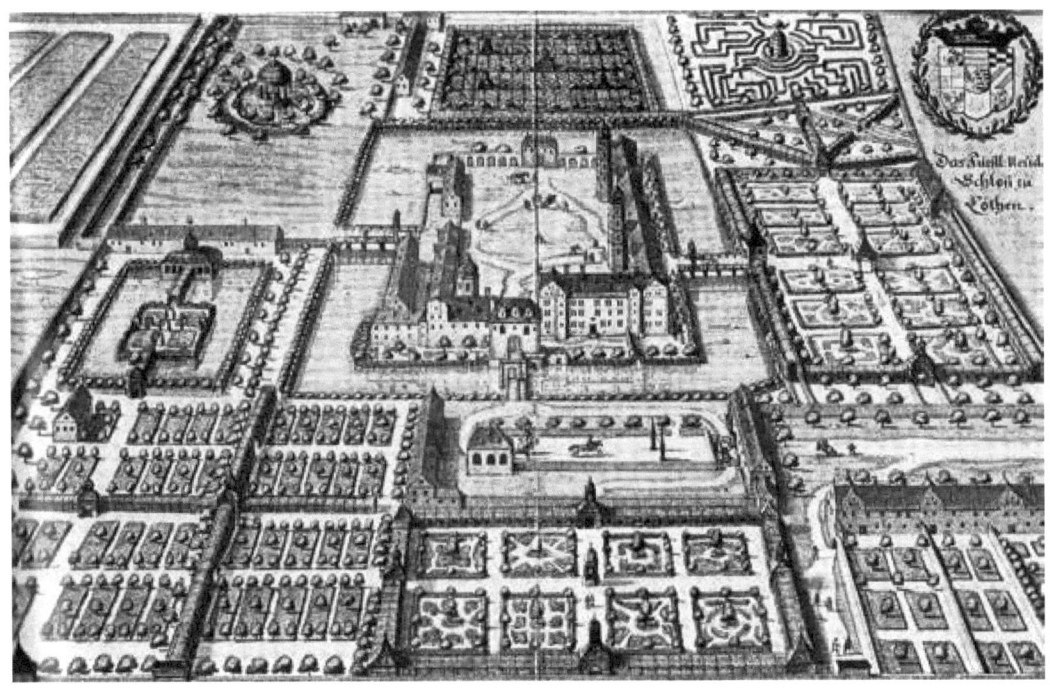

Köthen - Palace of Prince Leopold

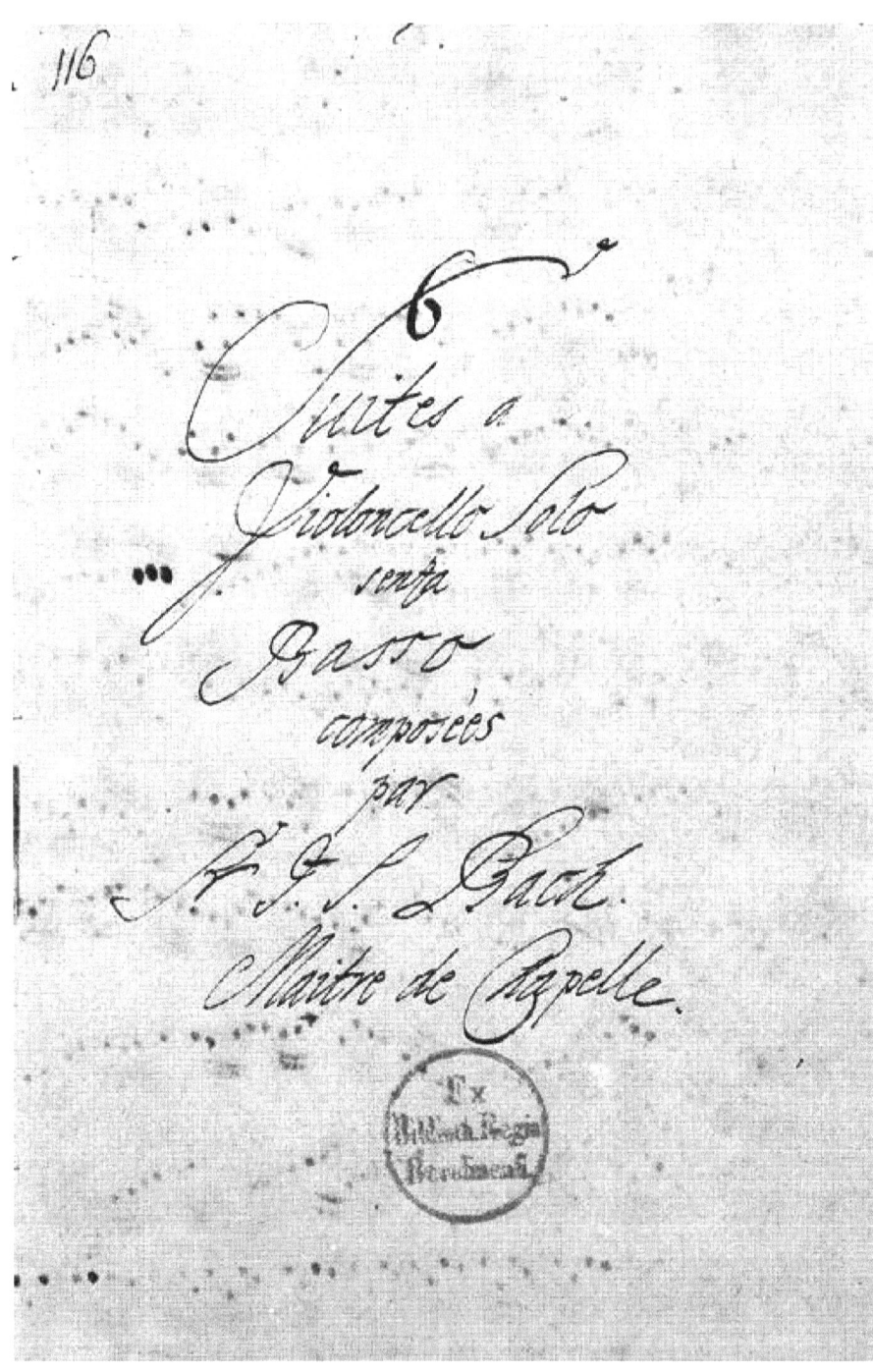

AN - Anna Magdalena

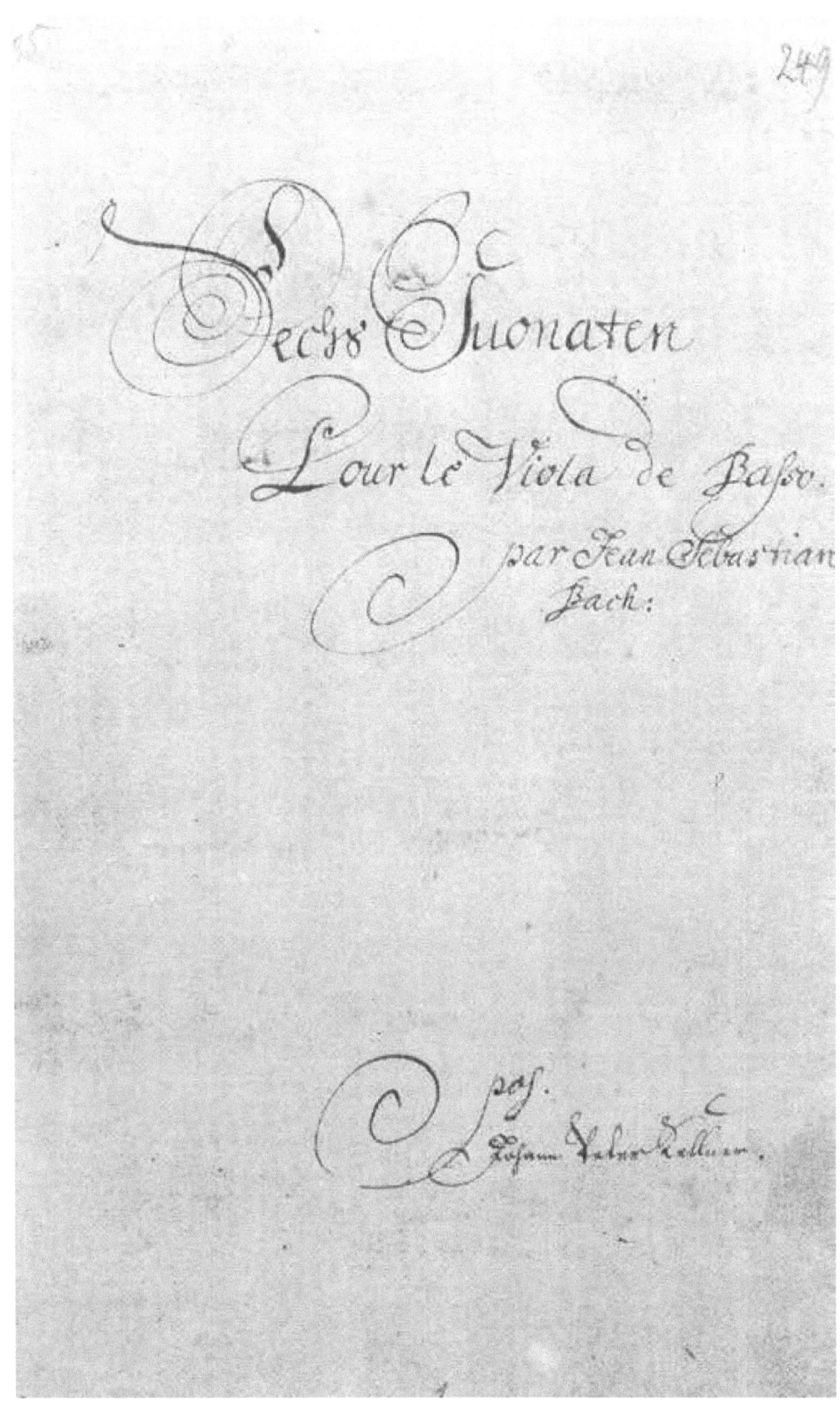

K - Johann Peter Kellner

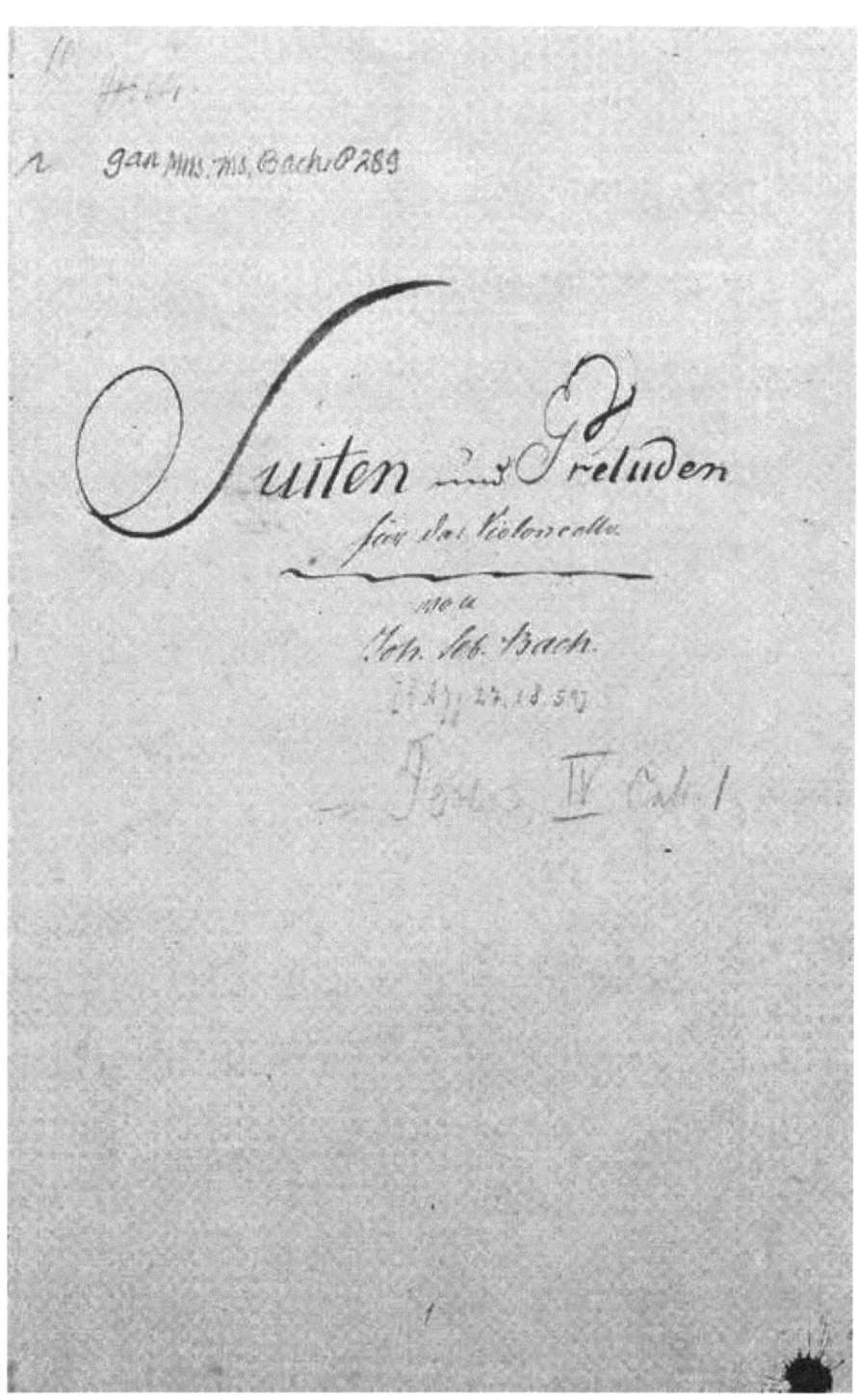

W - German Copy / Westphal?
2nd half 18th Century

AU - Austrian/German Copy 2nd half 18th Century

First page of J.S.Bach's Lute Suite Ms. after the 5th solo Cello Suite

Playing Bach

Some cellists have difficulties in performing J.S. Bach's Suites:
"We don't swim well in the pool of Bach's ideas"…

One famous elderly cellist, before recording the Suites ("my Last Chance") told me: "I really don't know how to play Bach".

Editions are plentiful, recordings are in abundance and moreover Bach is probably the most clear-minded composer of them all.

So what is the dilemma?

Since his writing is so ornamental, can it be that we have difficulties in separating his main statements from their ornamentation, as if every note is of the same importance?

Or is it because in his cello suites Bach didn't specify any tempi or dynamics, only bowings and few dots? Bach did use rich tempi and dynamic vocabulary in many of his other works.

Trusting one's intuition, strong as it is, without going into the syntax, meter and architectonic conception a player renders a personal portrayal which often lacks a convincing conceptual performance.

What is presented here aims to encourage further thinking, not only about the "how" but also about the "why".

Argument

A performer breathes life into a written musical work. It is always a recreative
process, a personal one. Even composers who perform their own works become
their own personal interpreters, not necessarily playing exactly what they have
written on paper. If only we could have heard J.S. Bach's playing. He was perhaps creating
anew, improvising, most likely changing some of his own written notes and rhythms,
and he probably never played the same way twice.

Many writers of the Baroque era wrote down their outlooks on and descriptions of the
playing practices of the time. Their "afterthoughts" and advice were meant to be guidelines
rules. It was an outcome of **their** understanding of the **living** art of the performance in that period.
Their information is most valuable in enriching our understanding. It is worth being
acquainted with and absorbing it. However a dogmatic/automatic following of these
mentioned "guidelines" to the letter is never the art itself.

The true art of performing is absorbing knowledge, trying to understand the composer's ideas,
recreating, breathing, using imagination, often breaking rules, employing personal intuition and
cultivated taste thus rendering a text full of colors and nuances which can never be put down on
paper. We know that the Baroque player did have much freedom in his rythmical and expressive
interpretation and there were probably accepted ways of performance.

The musical text, presented here, tries to open a way for further insight to the "anatomy" of Bach's
language and architectonic concept. The performer's mind, talent and imagination may then
recreate a convincing interpretation.

**There are endless ways of interpreting and editing Bach's cello suites, since his MS is
missing and publishing speculative and arbitrary text as urtext borders on the
absurd. In the four copies of the cello suites, and the lute version of the 5th Suite, there
are very many variations of bowings, notes, embellishments, rhythms etc.**

**This edition does not seek, ultimately, dogmatic academic musical solutions or merely instrumental
ways of performance or an artificial speculative Baroque sound reconstruction.
It looks for meaningful musical renderings, for taste, for the creations of a logical and
imaginative mind.**

**Bach would have probably liked to hear his masterful form, his phrase-interactions, his
harmonic interplays and many other aspects brought artistically to the fore.
Editions can help with this.**

Introduction

The idea of this work arose after meeting many musicians, artists, great young talents, students and music lovers all of them trying to understand Bach's language and ideas more clearly. This work is for them. It is the result of years of playing and teaching the Bach suites, years of studying and listening.

Editions of the suites, starting 1824, direct you "how" to play the suites (many times with personal bowings, fingerings, dynamics, metronome marks, etc.). The player-editor seldom explains "why". Some great artists like Alexanian, Mainardi, and Tortelier did try to clarify and articulate their own personal conceptions. The Bach-Gesellschaft edition (1879) did not have the advantage of the information we have today.

J.S.Bach's Ms is lost. There are four copies in existence. Two of the copies are from Bach's time, the one made by Bach's wife Anna Magdalena (1701 – 1760) and the other by J.J Kellner (1705 – 1772) who worked with Bach and copied many of his works. The two other copies are from later 18th century dates. All the four copies were published in facsimile edition by Baerenreiter, 1991.

The four copies are far from being the same. Could another early MS may have existed? Anna Magdalena's copy of J.S.Bach's violin solo works (also Kellner's) differs from his own existing MS with inaccuracies which led us to doubt whether to rely solely on their copies of the cello suites (both Anna Magdalena and Kellner were not string players!) - See introduction Bowings.
Is it possible that some copyists added their own acquired understandings, which they knew or heard from Bach? (i.e. Kellner)? It is probable that the later copyists changed their bowings when they changed their way of holding the bow from the hand "under the bow" like the Viola da Gamba to the hand "on the bow" and fit their bowings to the new way of holding.

The introductory thoughts and the remarks for each suite serve as information concerning J.S.Bach's works and Baroque usage, and together with the remarks in the musical text aim to introduce a succinct examination of Bach's language and ideas and also a suggestive (not binding) way of performing. There is no intention to "sophisticate" (or on the other hand to "simplify") Bach's extraordinarily clear-minded writing. But his music is vastly ornamented and has deeper layers. Discovering them, finding meanings and nuances of thought, only enriches our understanding and gives alternatives to choose from. They suggest a concept.

The suggested musical performance text (based mainly on AN) is not a "recipe" for **t h e** way to perform the suites. It should be tested, absorbed and not be demonstrated exaggeratedly since the art of playing bath is not the art of advertisement, of highly enlarge contrasting contours.

The text, syntax in rhetorics, should be well articulated and nuanced with musical logic, taste and imagination to be rendered in a natural-flowing in uncomplicated way.

The editor's suggested versions for performance, the result of years of developed taste and experience, offers the player some varieties from the other copies to recreate from.

Everything here is only a thesis, not a final version, since in the real art of interpretation doubts exist and there is no end to new discoveries. We constantly change and so does our approach to Bach's music. This is probably why Pablo Casals, who constantly changed his tempi, bowings etc., when he was asked, being over eighty - after countless performances and one recording - to edit the suites replied: "I am not ripe for it yet".

**The abbreviation signs
for the copies are:**

AN	Anna Magdalena (1701-1760)
K	Johann Peter Kellner (1705-1772)
W	Late German copy? Johann Christoph Westphal? (1727-1799)
AU	Late German copy? Austrian copy?
L	The lute version of the 5th suite

Thoughts and remarks

Voices: More "voices" are embodied in the one-stave writing of J.S.Bach's cello suites:

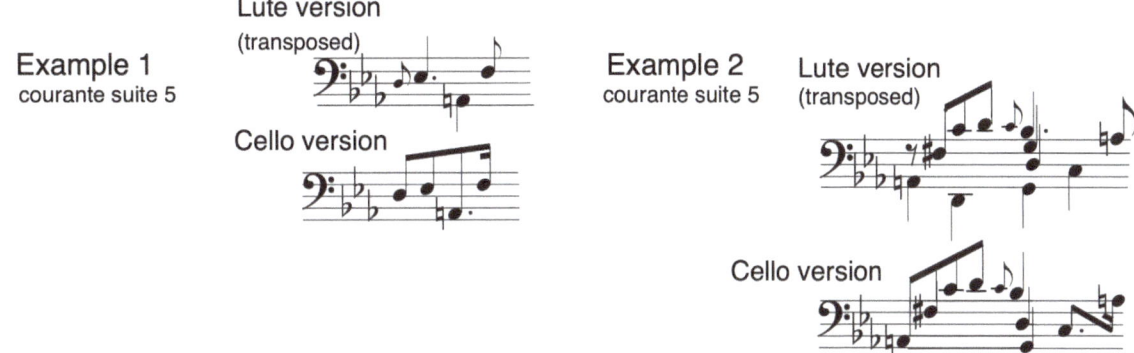

Example 1
courante suite 5

Lute version
(transposed)
Cello version

Example 2
courante suite 5

Lute version
(transposed)
Cello version

Here are more examples of Bach's two-dimensional way of writing:

Example 3
Allemande suite 1

another voice
20
one voice

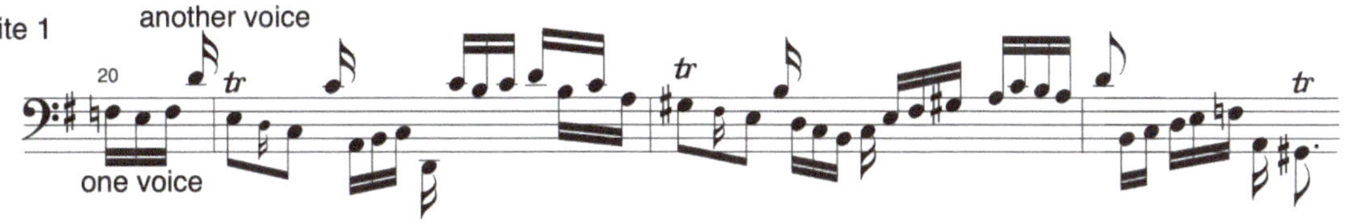

Example 4
Allemande suite 1

25

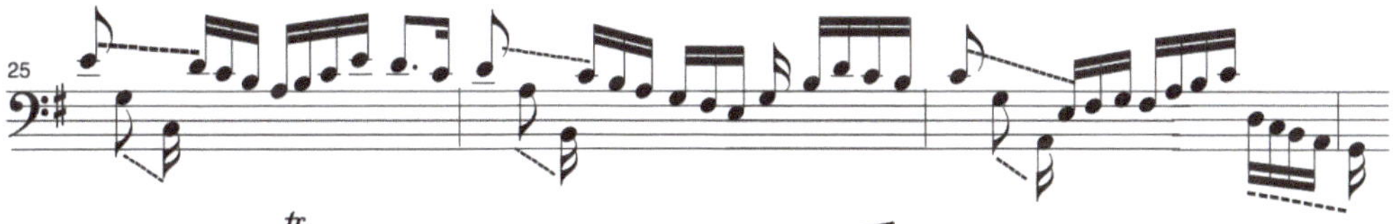

Example 5
Sarabande suite 2

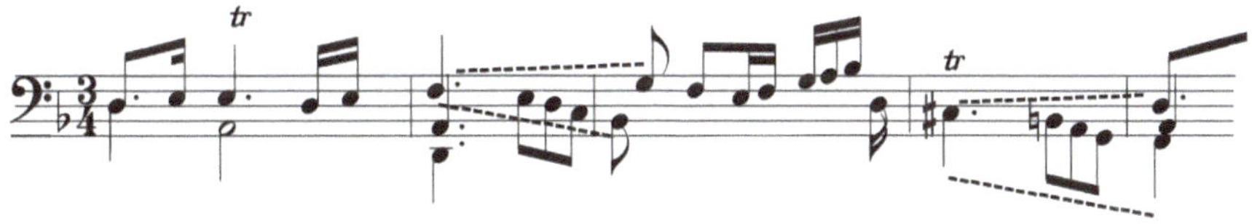

Example 6
Bouree suite 3

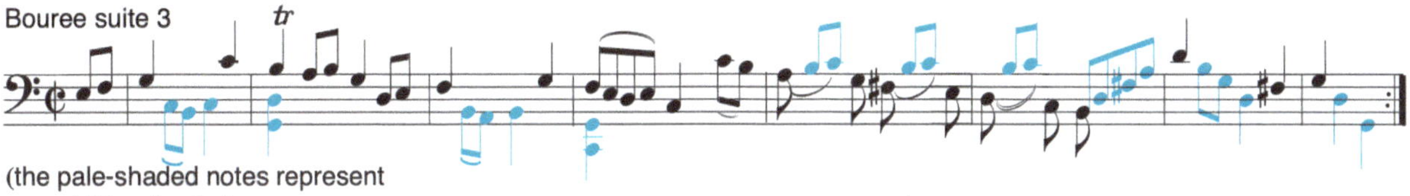

(the pale-shaded notes represent an additional voice)

Example 7
Gigue suite 4

5

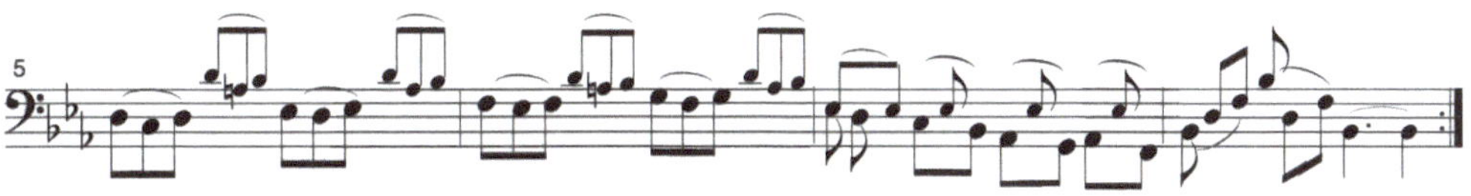

Example 8
Prelude suite 6

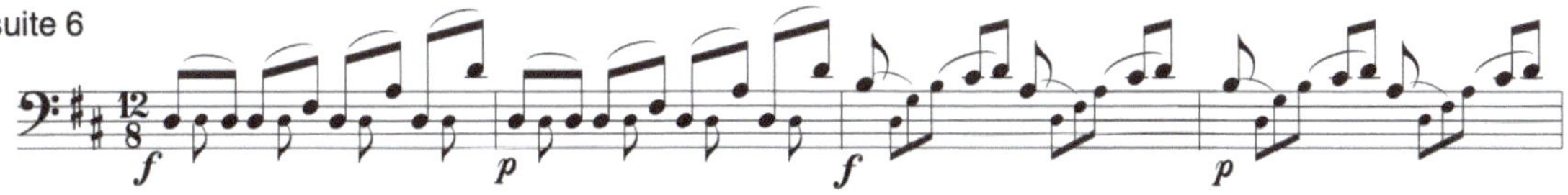

Main statements and ornamental connections: Bach's writing is ornamental
His main statements are mostly followed by ornamental connections:

Meter: The rhythmical undercurrent of every piece of music is its pulse (we define the counted pulses in a bar as beats). Music, like poetry, breathes meaningfully by recurring groups of pulses. This will be defined <u>here</u> as meter. These meter-groups have stressed and unstressed beats. The first beat is more "weighty" while the other beats are more "relaxed". First beats can be denoted by stronger articulation (not necessarily an accent!) or by staying a tiny bit longer on them. The stressed-articulated beat will be marked by the sign ⌣ . Meter is a prime element in Bach's music.
Here are some examples:

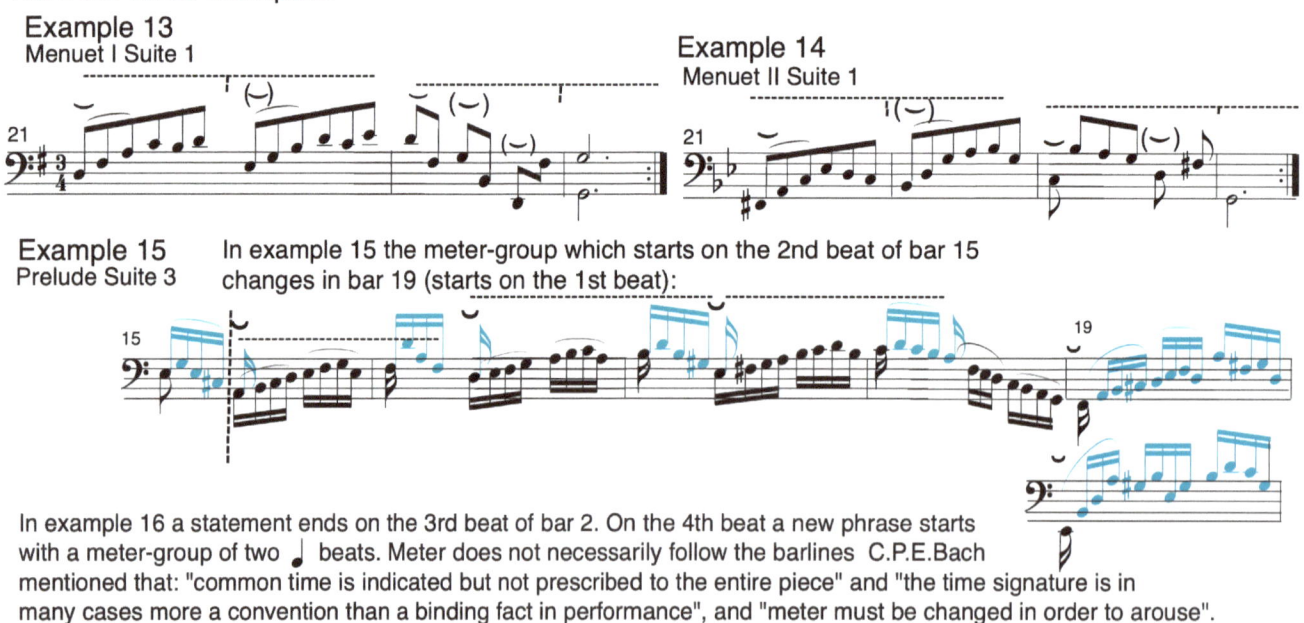

In example 16 a statement ends on the 3rd beat of bar 2. On the 4th beat a new phrase starts with a meter-group of two ♩ beats. Meter does not necessarily follow the barlines C.P.E.Bach mentioned that: "common time is indicated but not prescribed to the entire piece" and "the time signature is in many cases more a convention than a binding fact in performance", and "meter must be changed in order to arouse".

Example 17
Allemande Suite 1

In example 17 a meter starts on the 4th beat of bar 19 where new entities of two ♩ groups appear. The meter again changes at the beginning of bar 22.

Meter in dances

In the 3/4 dances there are larger meter-groups of two-bars' units. The first bar seems to be more "active" while the second one is more "passive" a sort of a "left and right" feeling. "...there are melodies in which it is clear that entire measures **are alternately heavy and light** (bold type is mine) so that one feels an entire measure to consist of one beat...then two measures must be necessary be set together to make a single one" [Johann Philipp Kirnberger (1721-1783) *"Die Kunst des reinen satzes"* (1771), Kirnberger studied with Bach]. Here are examples:

Example 18
Menuet I suite I

Example 19
Courante suite 3

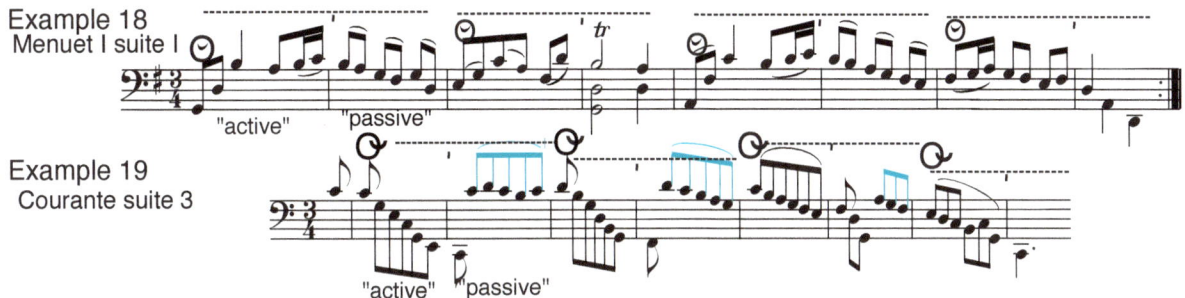

Tempo. What is a "right" tempo? Can we measure it? Can we create rules for it? The issue of tempo was already discussed in Bach's time, i.e. J.J.Quantz, C.P.E.Bach, and in our time Rothchild (controversial), Neumann and others. All were trying to find ways, outlooks, perception and concept in regard to tempo in the Baroque. Absorbing some of these writers' ideas, being convinced by a certain concept or just trusting one's own taste, logic and intuition a performer's choice of tempo will always be personal.

When a great artist convinces us with his performance and relays the text meaningfully with the choice of pulse and pace that seems to fit the contents which sounds like a real living organism, is it a "right" tempo? It is a matter of "...flexibility of the time, which is beaten now slowly now quickly and even held in the air, to match the expression of the music" (Frescobaldi's written introduction to his toccatas which Bach copied in full with its verbal text). For the Baroque player selecting a tempo, so it seems, was probably common knowledge and practice at that time (there were probably "accepted" tempi, more or less, for the dances!). J.S.Bach "...He have learnt the difference of time...no one can inculcate a knowledge of time at once. This must, however, be noticed, that in the present day one single kind of time is indicated in two ways, thus **C, 2**..." a dictate to Kellner who was a student of Bach).

Let us examine some elements which may help the choice of tempo.

One important factor is that In principle there is always a basic fundament. The rhythmical undercurrent of every piece of music is its pulse. A composer selects his basic pulse carefully. Bach writes in ♪ notes (example 17 above) or in ♪ notes (example 19) or in ♩ notes (i.e. sarabandes) thus advices us on his choice of a pulse resulting in choice of pace. Two examples:

Example 20
Prelude suite 4
written

If it is played too fast it will sound as if it was written

Example 21
Courante suite 3
written

If it is played too fast it will sound as if it was written

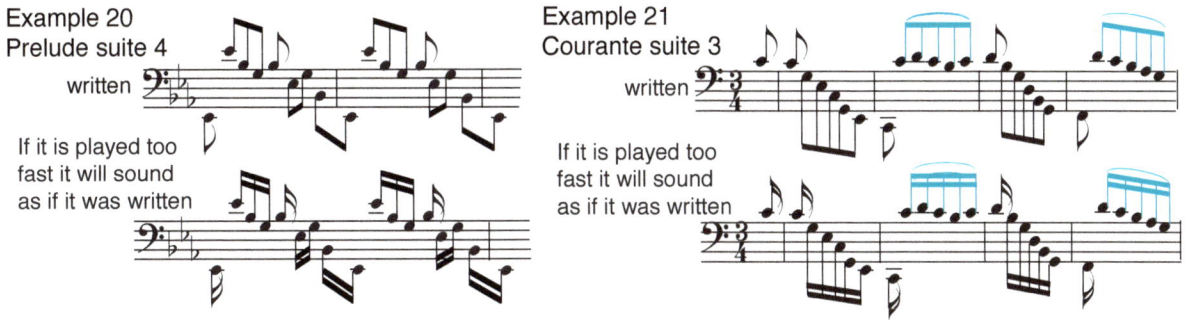

Bach chose his fastest rhythm-pulses thoughtfully and one can find a pace accordingly and keep the character and the mood of the piece and its charm (too fast a tempo creates virtuosic tension which often lacks charm). Every movement should "breathe naturally", have its own character and flair and will also function better as a part of the suite as a whole.

Another factor is the discovery of Bach's pulse-beats (sometimes "hidden"). It may help the personal choice of a "right" tempo:

Example 22
Prelude suite 5

One notices in bar 3 the "heavy" ♩ pace and the ♩ pulse

(This ♩ pulse will eventually equal probably a bar of 3/8 in the fugue ♩ = ♩.)

Another factor is the perception and understanding of the syntax thus allowing the text to breathe:

The grasp of a whole statement (with its parts) in examples 23 and 24 will create a framework for a choice of tempo.

Example 23
Allemande suite 2

Example 24
Allemande suite 6

Furthermore a performer should articulate very distinctly and render a text in a clear and meaningful way retaining its charm and flair.

The issue of ₵ (alla breve) is an ambigous, controversial and a speculative one. In the cello suites we find few times that movements are marked in some copies ₵ and in others C. One of the reasons (in the later copies) has to do with the trend in the second half of the 18th century not to use the ₵. The ₵ may also point out and result in the idea of grasping larger units of syntax in the text (i.e. allemande in a meter of two! see the following example 25). It is our concept that ₵ is not concerned basically with tempi or speed directions.

Example 25
Allemande suite 1

One can sense the half bars's units.

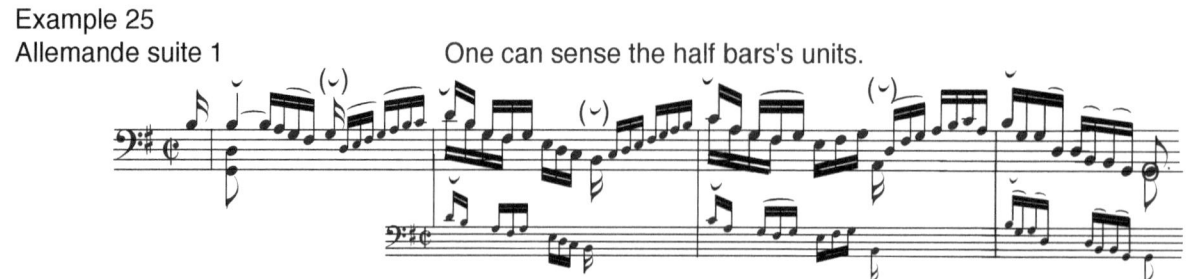

Articulation is the clear pronunciation of the rhetorical lines. In our musical text the signs ⌐ or ⌊ denote the beginning of a phrase or a statement (not necessary an accent), as we do with our lips or tongue when we try to speak clearly. C.P.E.Bach said of his father: "In his way of playing he seemed to be talking all the time". J.J.Quantz writes: "Musical manner of performance may be compared with the delivery of an orator". Later J.N.Forkel (who was very friendly with C.P.E.) writes about J.S.Bach:"...playing his own music...every piece sounded in his hands like a speech".

The articulation signs do not have to follow the meter they only contribute to the clarity of speech.

Example 26
Allemande suite 1

etc.

The signs ⌐ or ⌐ denote the end of a phrase or a statement. Often we find in Bach's music an end-note of a phrase which functions as a beginning of a new phrase:

Example 27
Prelude suite 1

The c# In bar 20 is the end of a descending line but this c# is also a beginning of a new statement. The descending line could be relaxed towards its end and the c# could be softer dynamically. However with this c#(no need for an accent) the energy surges immediately forward.

In example 28 the marked syntax groups are separate entities! and should be so articulated. But they should pulse within the frame of the existing time-beats.

Example 28
Prelude suite 1

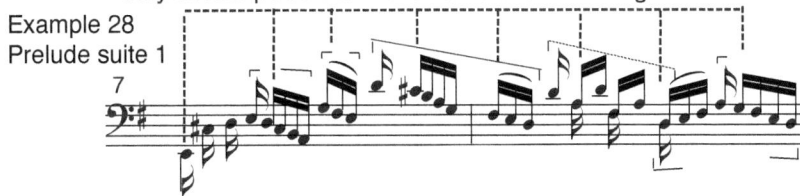

Performance: Quantz: "Some move the bow as is customary on the viola da gamba, that is, instead of a down stroke from right to left for the principal notes, they make up-strokes from left to right, beginning with the tip of the bow. Others begin their stroke with the lowest part of the bow. This later method is customary among the Italians, and produces a better effect..."
There were arched cello bows in Bach's time but there were also down-curved cello bows (like ours today). Charles Burney wrote (as late as 1773 !): "M.Graudel, a violoncello performer in the king's band played a concerto...It was well enough executed, though in the **old manner with the hand under the bow**" (bold type is mine).

Whichever way the bow was held its stroke and articulation were probably done mostly by an arm movement. It is not our nowadays conception of an "intensive" sustained sound.
Notes and phrases were probably articulated more with the arm using an initial faster speed and more bow, which "relaxes" later, like switching on the light which stays afterwards. This manner uses various speeds of the bow also different lengths of it.

Articulation can use more bow or less bow

Example 29
Prelude suite 5

the lower 2nd voice can have a softer nuance by using a shade of less bow.

Example 30
Allemande suite 1

In example 31 we can use less bow on the "not so important" notes (2nd, 3rd and 4th notes of every bar, smaller type) and also on the repeated notes at the end of the bars.

Example 31
Prelude suite 3

In example 32 in bars 1-2 every 2nd note of the triplets can have less bow. The p bars (bars 2, 4 etc.) can have less bow than the f bars (bars 1, 3). The same with the main voice and the "accompaniment" in bars 3-4. In bars 5-7 one can imagine the first notes of the bars as longer notes g (o - bar 5), f# (o - bar 6) then e (d) and d (d - bar 7) and one can stay longer on the circled notes and articulate the marked ones.

Example 32
Prelude suite 6

Bowings: What are the "right" bowings in the cello suites? Should we rely on any particular copy? AN had J.S Bach's Ms to copy from. Kellner was there too. However both AN and K had many inaccuracies. If we i.e. compare AN copy of Bach's solo violin works with Bach's own Ms (which exists) we find many differences in bowings, like in the following examples:

Example 33
Adagio 1st Sonate for Violin Solo:

In examples 33a and 33c in AN there are incomplete slurs. Suppose a similar example like 30c (AN version) was in AN's copy of the cello suites. It would have been accepted by many as a *fait accompli*, one separate note and three slurred ones! Should we accept everything in An's copy to the letter? Should we infer from her irregularities that J.S.Bach meant to write as many varieties of bowings as possible (see "Bach, the fencing master" by Anner Bylsma). Does it make sense?

While relying on AN's bowings it is advisable to consult also the other copies rather than accepting blindly, *a priori*, just one copy and dismiss the others.

Example 34
Prelude suite 6

Did AN definitely wanted unslurred notes in the 3rd beat of the 1st bar? (in bars 11-14 she wrote all the bowings! except one).

Bach's bowings essentially articulate the syntax and express musical charecteristics and contrasts. They are not just technical-executional directions (many times, of course, they are both). Bowings can be changed as long as the result does not distort Bach's syntax, disregard the meter or disturb the natural flow of the music. J.J.Quantz: "...it is necessary to avoid sluring notes which ought to be detached and detaching notes which ought to be slurred". The issue of instrumental comfort and what "sounds" better is very important and many times unavoidable. But the choice of bowings ought to be musically dictated with logic, taste and imagination.

Dotted rhythm: In the written vocabulary of Bach's time there were no double-dotted rhythms. However in practice ♩· ♪ was played approximately as ♩·· ♪ and ♪· ♪ as ♪·· ♪ also ♩· ♪♪♪♪ as ♩· ♪♪♪♪ but not automatically every time and not mathematically exact.

C.P.E.Bach (1759): "Short notes which follow dotted ones are always shorter in execution than their notated length" and "Short notes, which follow dotted ones, are...played more rapidly than their notation indicates". However Quantz writes (1751): "...the time of the short notes after the dots cannot actually be fixed with complete exactness".

And again C.P.E.Bach: "...proper exactness is often lacking in the notation of dotted notes, a general rule of performance has been established which, however, has many exceptions. According to this rule, the notes which follow the dots are to be played in the most rapid manner; and often they should be. But sometimes...a modification of the rule is required...if only one kind of execution is adopted as the basic principle of performance, the other kinds will be lost." Certain "rules" were not followed in actual performance leaving the choice to the player's taste and imagination. Here is a written rhythmical variation in Bach's own writing:

Example 35
Prelude suite 5

Also it is possible to play:
Example 36 Sarabande suite 3   Example 37 Sarabande suite 2   **Example 38 Allemande suite 1** it is possible (approximately)
(see introduction page 10 example 40)

All these variations should not be executed automatically every time, they should match the musical contents tastefully.

Bach himself wrote also different rhythmical versions of the same work, i.e. the "French overture" for the cembalo (example 39). In the later version (1735) he put the actual rhythms to be played :

Example 39 BWV 831a

Besides the change of key we notice the rhythm flexibility in the 1735 version. Bach didn't write double-dotted rhythm in the 1733 version. But we notice in the middle and at the end of bar 3 the ♪ notes.

Should one play at the end of bars 12 and 13 also a double-dotted rhythms?

An important example of rhythmical application in performance in the allemande of the 5th suite of the lute version, where Bach himself wrote the "double-dotted" rhythms (bars 1-2 and 6-7). We can also see the flexible, not automatic, use of it in bars 10, 11!

Example 40
Allemande suite 5

Example 41 Sarabande suite 1

Ornamentation: Exececution of the ornaments depends on the right information, personal taste and concept. Addition of ornamental lines to the existing text, especially in the repeats, similar to the doubles Bach wrote in his keyboard suites or in some of the solo violin works is speculative.
C.P.E.Bach wrote his cello concerti in two more versions for the flute and for the cembalo.
The cello part i.e. in the A major concerto, in the slow movement, has almost no ornaments while the cembalo part is full of them. Should we adorn the cello part with the harpsichord's ornamental lines? There is no definite answer. There are some embellishments in the copies, which can be used in the repeats, but these are not added ornamental lines! Do the cello suites need more ornamental lines? Do we have space for them? Can we do it as well as Bach?

Inequality: Much was written about the rhythmical inequality in the playing in the Baroque period. Couperin wrote: " we notate otherwise than we perform...we perform as dotted a succession of ♪ notes... yet we notate them as equal." Does the French mode apply also to the German way of playing? Quantz:"...the quickest notes in...moderate tempo, or...in Adagio...must be played a little unequally...if the ♪ notes...are played slowly with the same value, they will not sound pleasing...Excepted from the rule, however, is...quick passage-work in a very fast tempo in which time does not permit unequal execution..." Bach himself in one of his violin concerti which he rewrote for the cembalo changed equal rhythmical notes to

We can apply the inequality in the Allemande of the 1st suite:

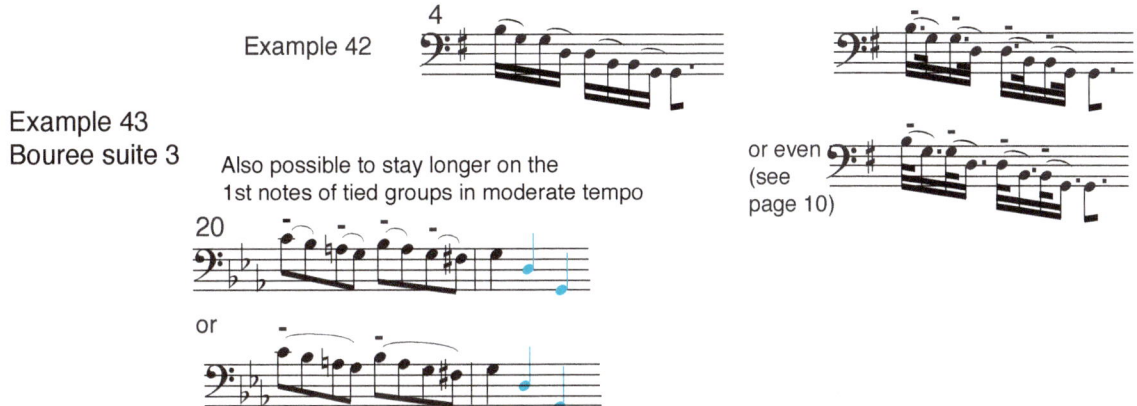

Example 42

**Example 43
Bouree suite 3**

Also possible to stay longer on the
1st notes of tied groups in moderate tempo

or even
(see
page 10)

This manner of playing may add charm and grace.

Bach's energy tides: The tides of musical energy are an essential part of any musical creation. We can try to draw charts which show clearly Bach's stream of energy:

Example 44 Prelude suite 1

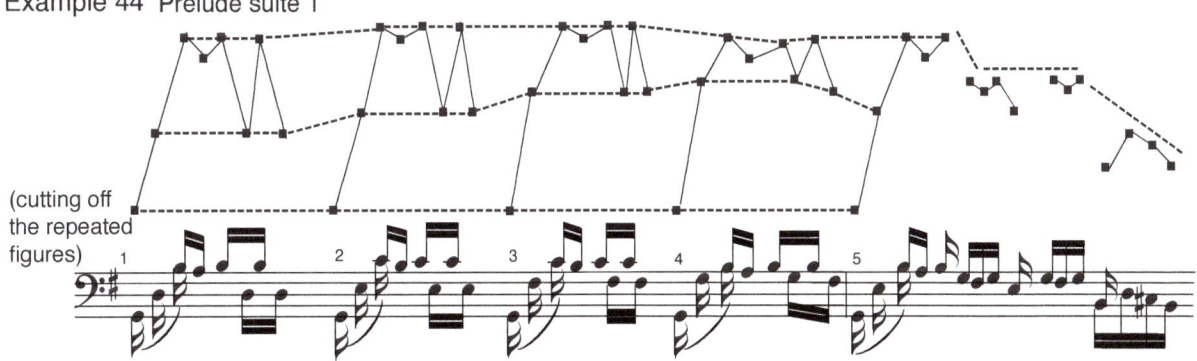

(cutting off the repeated figures)

In example 44 we can detect the middle and upper "voices" rising and abating with the harmonic tension. The upper "voice" descending with the harmonic relaxation. We can also see the contrast between the first 4 bars and the not-broken-chordal line going down at bar 5.

Example 45 Prelude suite 1

Bach shortens his 4 bars' dual groups of broken chords (bars 1-4) to one bar (bar 7), while the non-broken-chordal line is enlarged to two-bars.

Horizon line: Bach's creative energy, his ideas, dictated his architectonic lines.
One can draw an imaginary "horizon line" which connects the highest notes of a piece, especially in the preludes similar to a line of spires in some gothic churches, where among many spires there exists a highest one, the climax! This "horizon line" may help us to follow his energy "tides":

Example 46
Prelude suite 1

This may serve as an energy-development guide which is different in the other preludes.

In the next example we can follow the "skyline" in the prelude to the 3rd suite from bar 37 noticing Bach's "four-dimentional" way of writing:

Example 47 Prelude suite 3

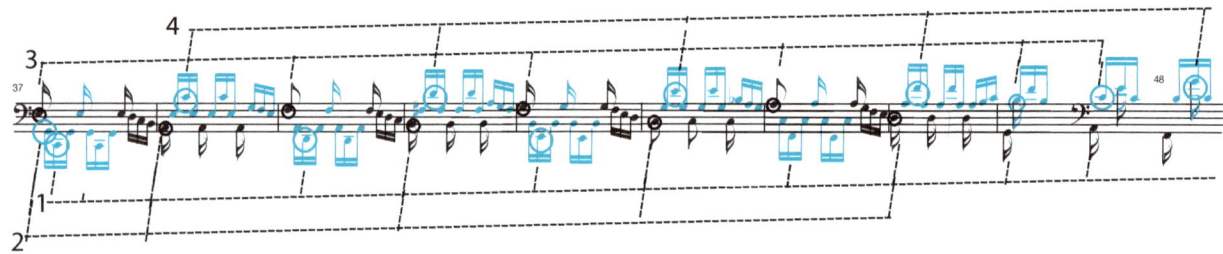

Continuity: Bach's music is moving constantly.

Example 48
Prelude suite 3

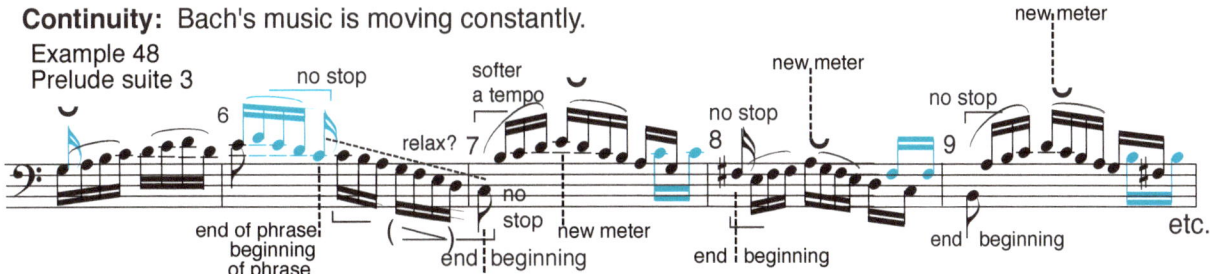

The lower c in the beginning of bar 7 is an end of a phrase but it is also an energy spark without break for a new beginning of a new phrase (AN copy specifies it by having a tie of the four notes). The same is in the beginning of bar 9 where the end-note b is also the beginning of a new energy. One can relax at the end of a statement, i.e. towards the lower c in bar 7 which can be the softest dynamically; but this c is a new spark in tempo (without a stop). This end-beginning on the same note is one of the basic elements of Bach's language.

Here are more examples:

Example 49
Prelude suite 2

Example 50
Allemande suite 2

The bass note of the chord is the end of a line while the upper note is the start of a new line.

In the following examples (51 and 52) the end notes of each small phrases are also the beginning of the next ones. The dynamic-agogic subtelty here calls for a softness of the first notes of the second, third and fourth phrases, but at the same time these notes initiate a new energy which start the new phrases!

Example 51
Allemande suite 4

Example 52
Allemande suite 1

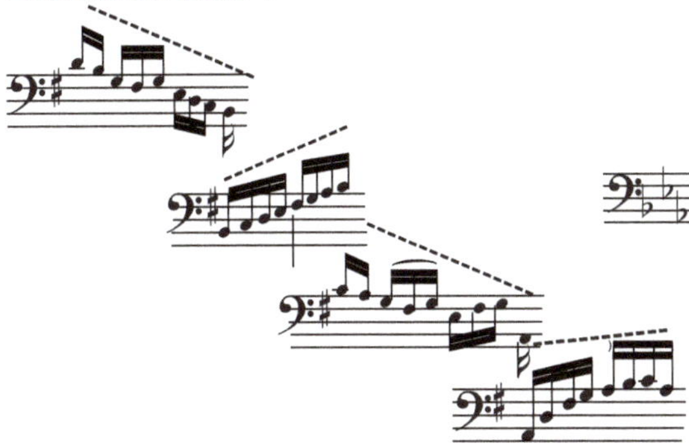

And the long phrase

And the long phrase

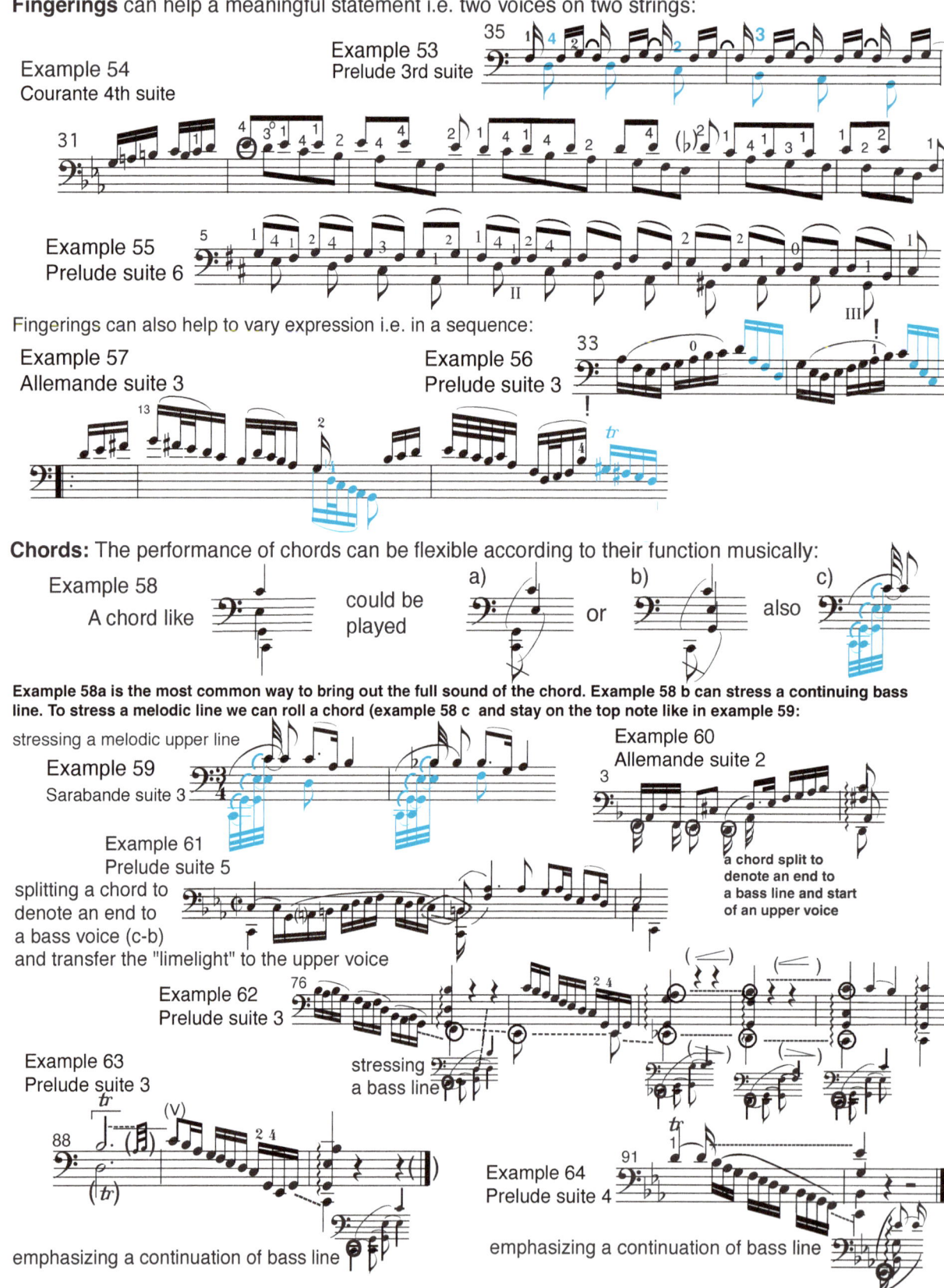

Dynamics: There are only few dynamics marks in the cello suites. But Bach uses in his works rich with varied dynamic vocabulary comprising *pianissimo, piu piano, piano, poco forte, mezo forte, forte* and more. In the performance of the cello suites the dynamic shades are left to the taste and the discretion of the player. There are several points to make:

a) Terraces, sequences and registers

The bars in example 65 constitute a long phrase with three sequences, in a form of three "terraces". Each terrace is one tone lower and is divided into two registers. All this can be expressed by subtle dynamics i.e each terrace slightly softer.

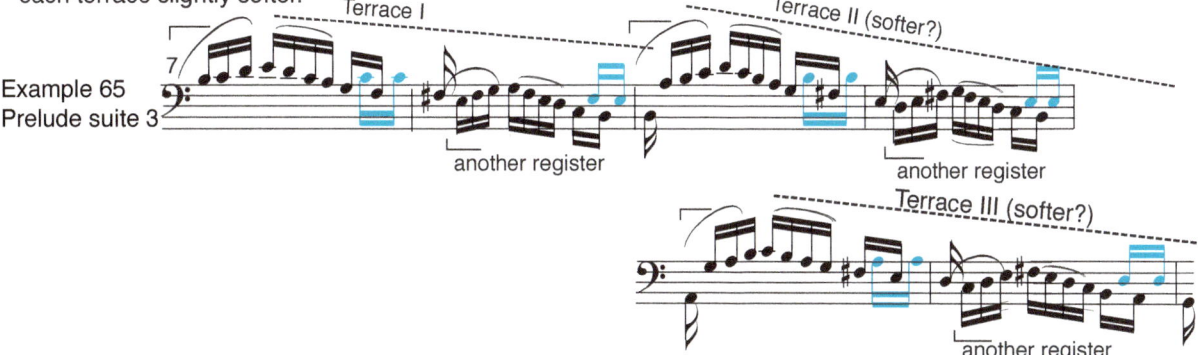

Example 65
Prelude suite 3

b) Group dynamics:
When energy grows or abates by sequences intensity (cresc. or dim.) develops by groups and not from note to note.

In example 66 there are descending bass-lines in each bar. Sequences are abating dynamically by the bars! (in addition there could be a tiny dim. at the end of each bar?

Example 66
Gigue suite 4

Bach creates in example 67 two-bars' groups then shortening them to one bar's units. Then a two-bars' group leading to bar 25. Group dynamics can be used here to arrive at the climax c in bar 25!

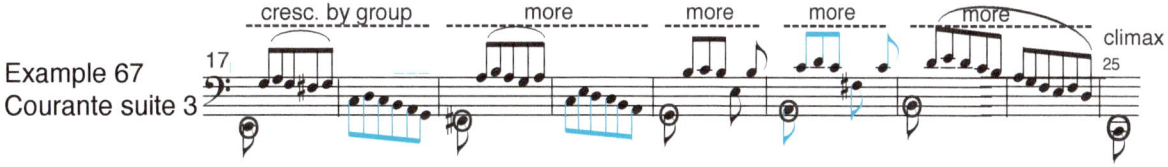

Example 67
Courante suite 3

Example 68
Courante suite 4   we can follow the groups and develop the dynamics accordingly:

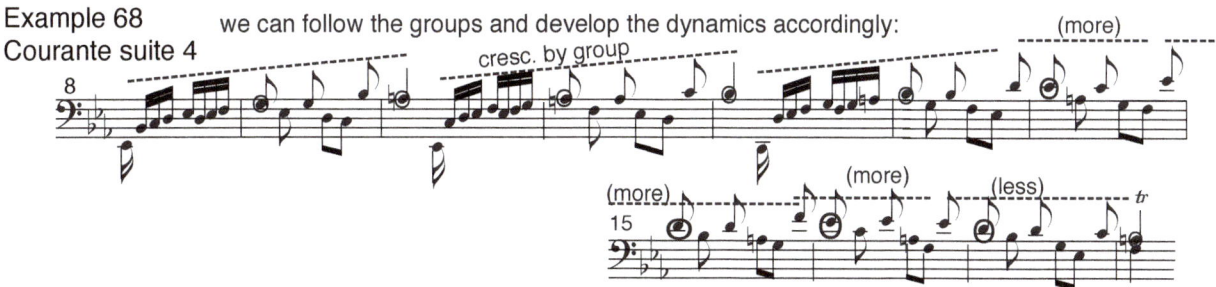

c) **Dynamic levels:** Sometimes in Bach's text there are two independant voices with two different levels of dynamics:

Example 69
Courante suite 1 — two voices, two levels of dynamics, one ascending the other constant,

In example 70 the bass line descends (bars 77-81) while the upper voice ascends (bars 79-81). The two dynamic levels can be projected by staying on the bass notes, arpeggiating the chord and staying on the upper notes.

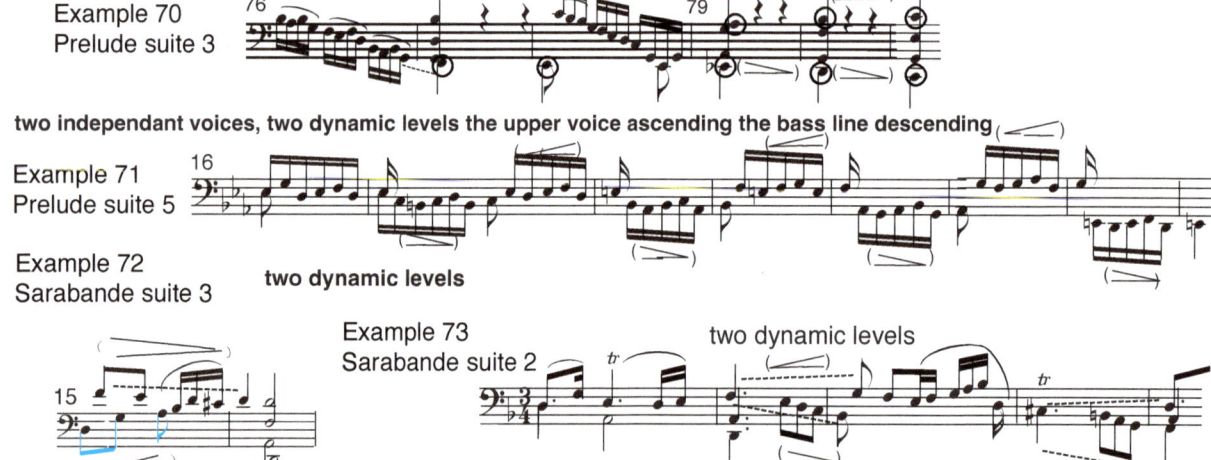
Example 70
Prelude suite 3

two independant voices, two dynamic levels the upper voice ascending the bass line descending

Example 71
Prelude suite 5

Example 72
Sarabande suite 3 — two dynamic levels

Example 73
Sarabande suite 2 — two dynamic levels

d) **Dynamics and the meter:** As was mentioned before the meter creates a meaningful "breathing" in music like a living organism. It is essential to preserve the meter without disrupting it by dynamics.

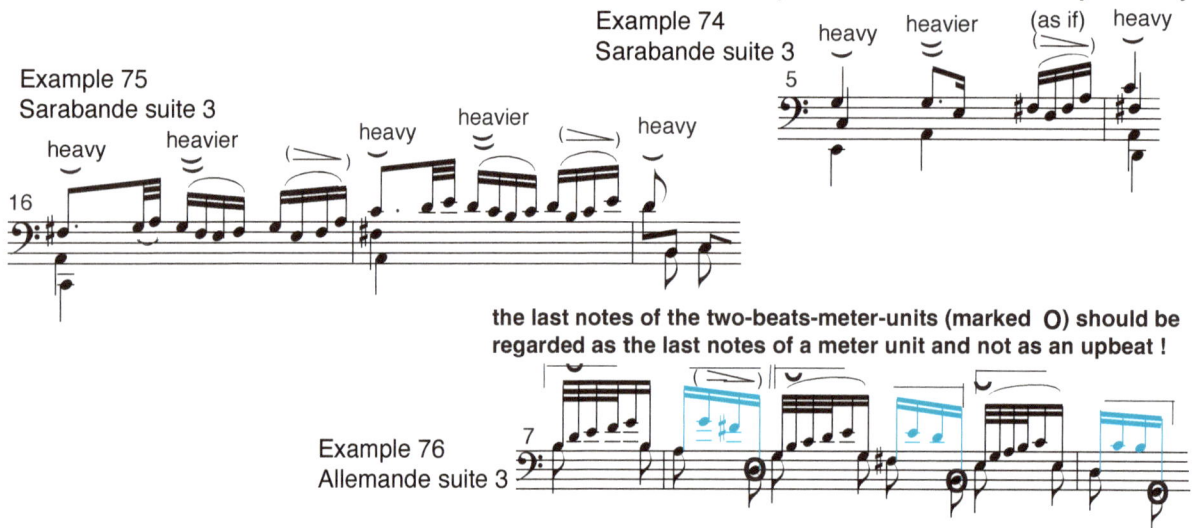

The 3rd beat shouldn't be an intentional upbeat. It could be softened dynamically.

Example 74
Sarabande suite 3

Example 75
Sarabande suite 3

the last notes of the two-beats-meter-units (marked O) should be regarded as the last notes of a meter unit and not as an upbeat !

Example 76
Allemande suite 3

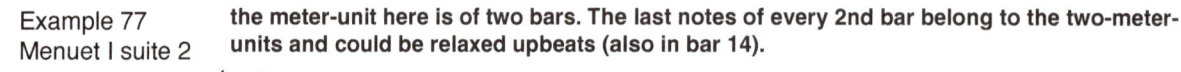
Example 77
Menuet I suite 2 — the meter-unit here is of two bars. The last notes of every 2nd bar belong to the two-meter-units and could be relaxed upbeats (also in bar 14).

Phrasing: In the art of rhetoric division, phrasing and articulation should not deviate from the natural pulse and pace in the playing of Bach's cello suites

Example 78 Allemande suite 1

The articulation, especially in the 2nd half of the bar, should be within the beats as marked:

Example 79
Prelude 4th suite

Since there is a repeated dual statement (similar to the prelude of the 1st suite) one can stay longer only on the 1st bass note of the 1st bar of the dual unit, the stressed note of the meter. The articulation on the 2nd note is within the beat!

Postscript:

When just an intuition recreates Bach's six suites - impressive as it is - something will be still missing.

All the information and thoughts in the **Introduction** and the remarks in the music text try to suggest more insight and to trigger some thinking towards a conception.
To quote again from the Argument on page 1: " the true art of playing is breathing, using imagination, often breaking rules, flourishing with personal taste and using colors and nuances which can never be put on paper ". All this on top of absorbing knowledge and trying to understand the composer's ideas.

Frederick Neumann writes: "The Baroque performer enjoyed vast latitude in interpretation of the score ...(using) an elastic treatment of rhythmic notation (and) guided by the "Affect" of a passage, he applied agogic accents, used rubato techniques of all kinds, varied the tempo, sharpened a rhythm here, softened it there. No rules governed this performance style its only law was musical instinct and arbitrary judgememt ".

There is a children's story where a boy was sent looking for a flower - the "golden-heart" one - to bring it to his mother as a cure for her grave illness. He had to cling on and hold a very thin silky thread, hardly noticable, which led him to that flower and the cure.
In every Bach's movement this silky thread is the binding stream of his creative energy. Not easily found. But finding and holding the thread eventually will bring out a meaningful convincing performance.

Suite I

BMW 1007

PRELUDE
ALLEMANDE
COURANTE
SARABANDE
MENUET I - MENUET II
GIGUE

The German prince Leopold of Anhalt-Köthen (1694 - 1728) who was an amateur viola da gamba player, hired musicians from North Germany to form his private orchestra in his castle. These musicians included both the famous viola da gamba player (Abel) and a cello player (Lienicke). Prince Leopold appointed J.S. Bach to be the Kappelmeister - director of music.

During his work in Köthen (1717 - 1723) Bach "discovered" the cello, which was at the time a newcomer as a solo instrument. Bach wrote the 1st suite in Köthen, and probably some or all of the other solo suites.

The adaption of the 5th suite for the Lute was written later in Leipzig.

Already in the first suite we can find Bach's two-dimensional way of writing., the meter's importance, the architectonic concept snd many other elements which appear in the later suites.

The slur over three notes (of a group of eight) is used more often by all the copies which are not consistant in their bowings. It is preferred here.
Staying on notes, articulation of circled notes only once in one unit.

The 1st prelude from the "Well tempered clavichord" has a similar architectonic design of harmonic broken-chords with dual statements throughout. The way Bach wrote it may show a sound concept:

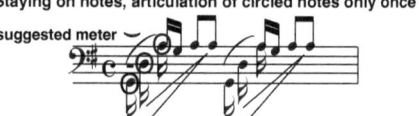

Prelude performance suggestion

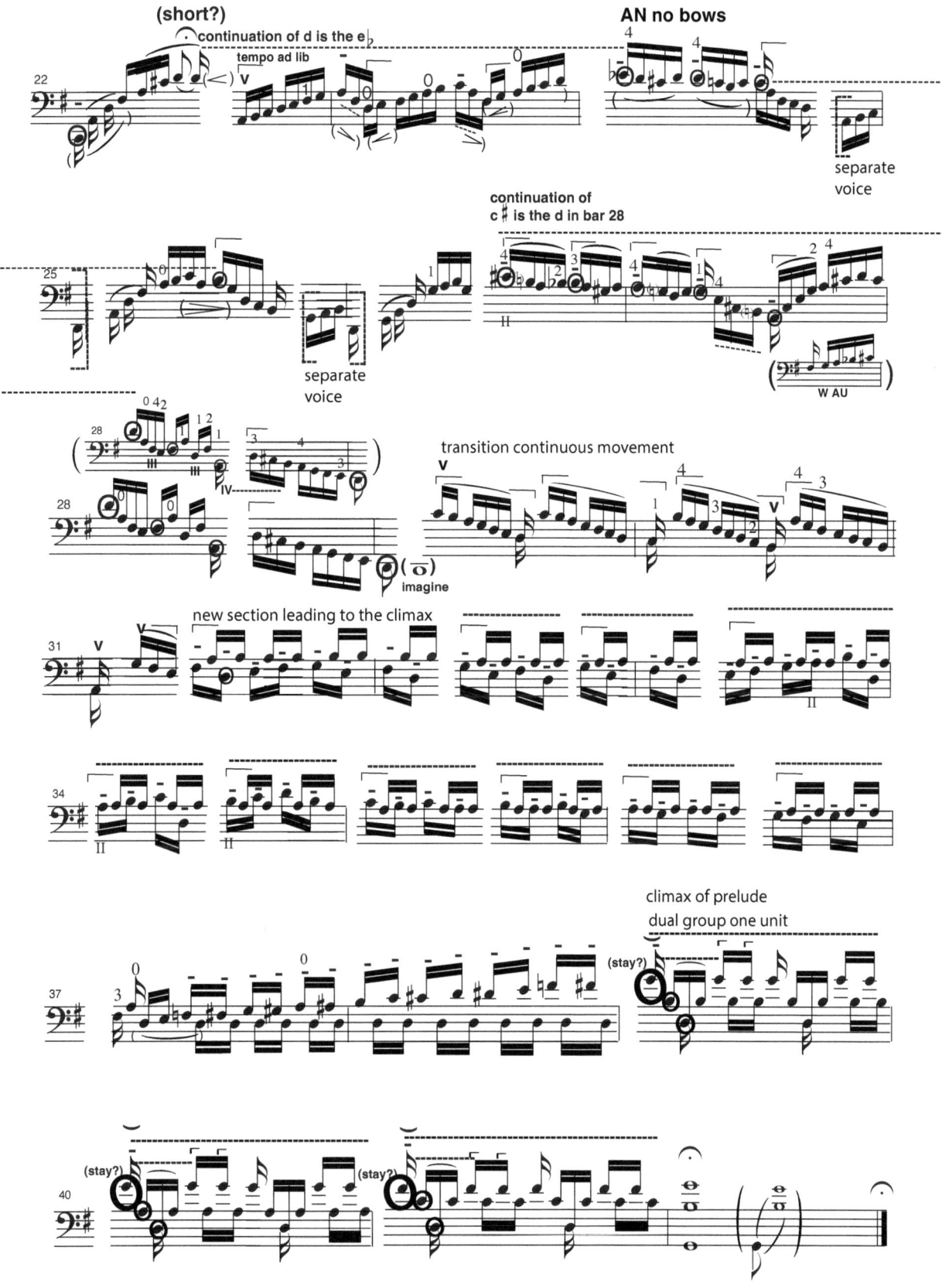

Allemande is of "serious and dignified" character with a singing quality. Here it is more recitative like.
The meter is in two half bars. The last note of the small phrases is also the beginning of the new ones, to be played in tempo.
Bowings are according to AN with some variations chosen from other copies in brackets.

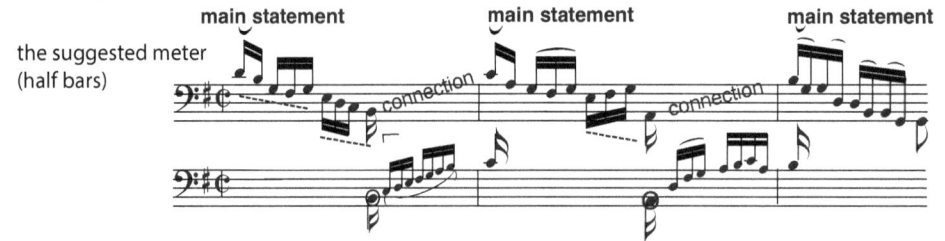

Allemande performance suggestion

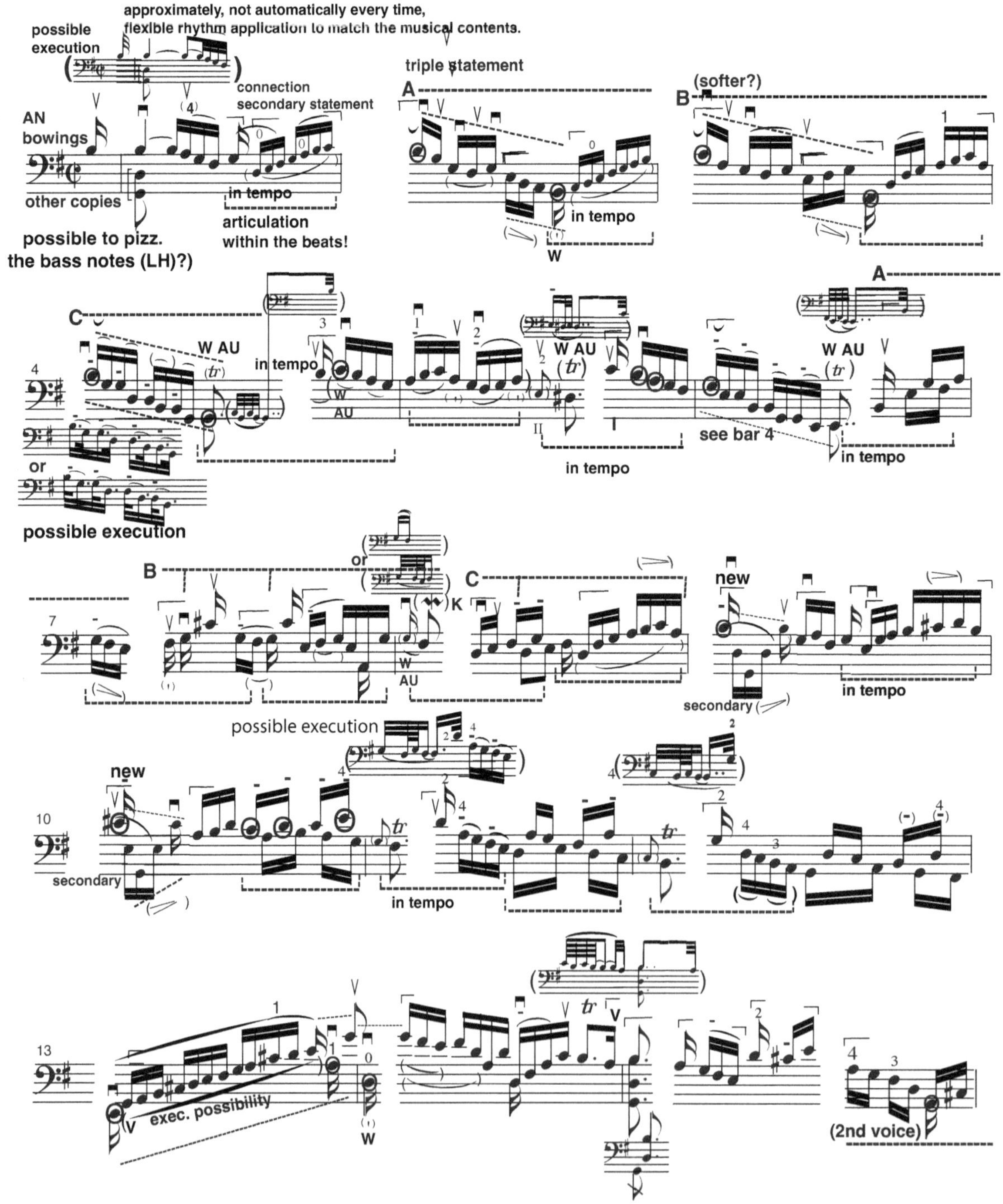

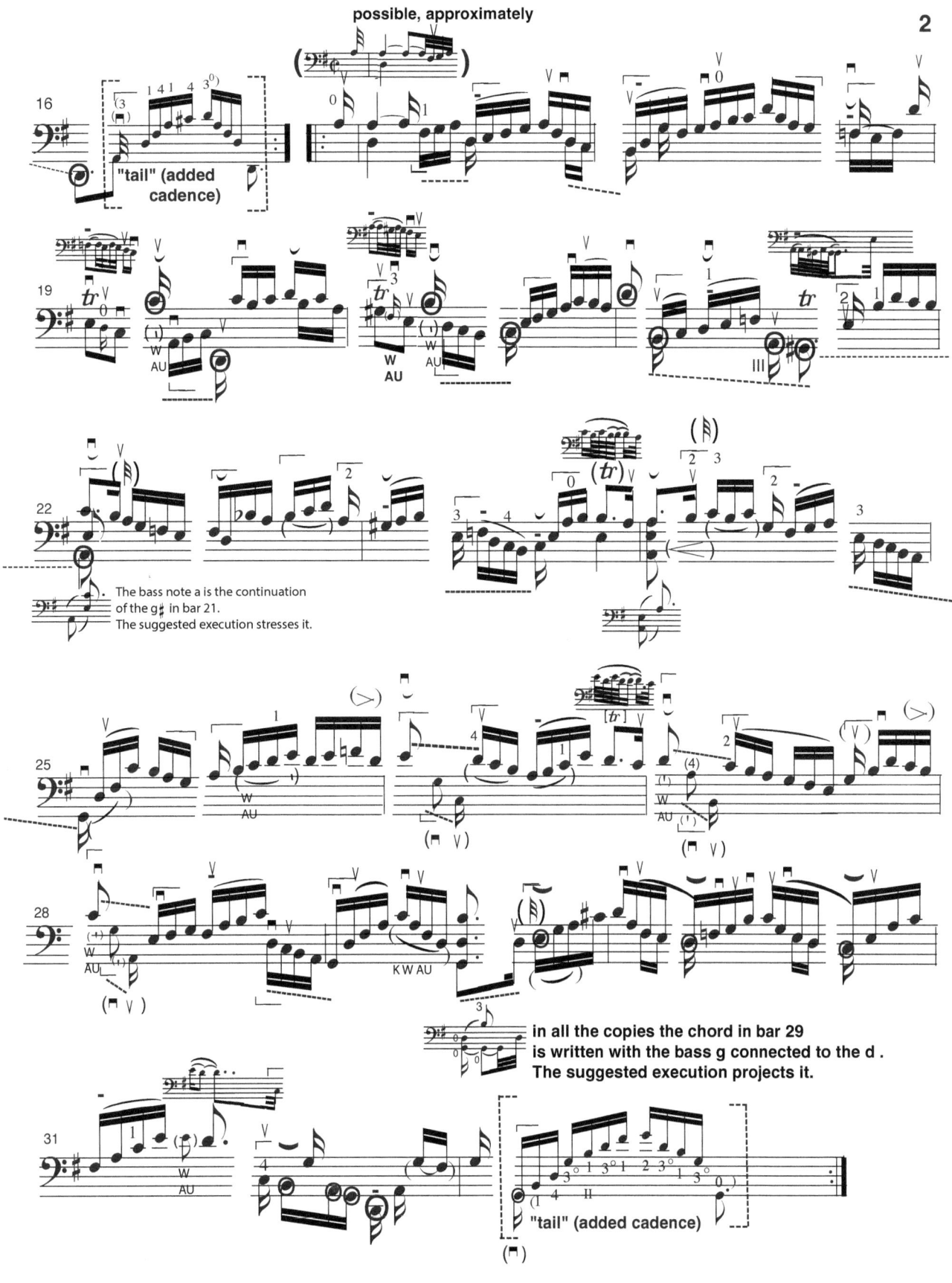

The suggested meter

Courante performance suggestion

A moderately fast courante. Two dimentional way of writing. The two voices, should be well articulated.

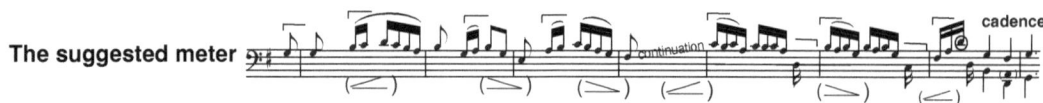

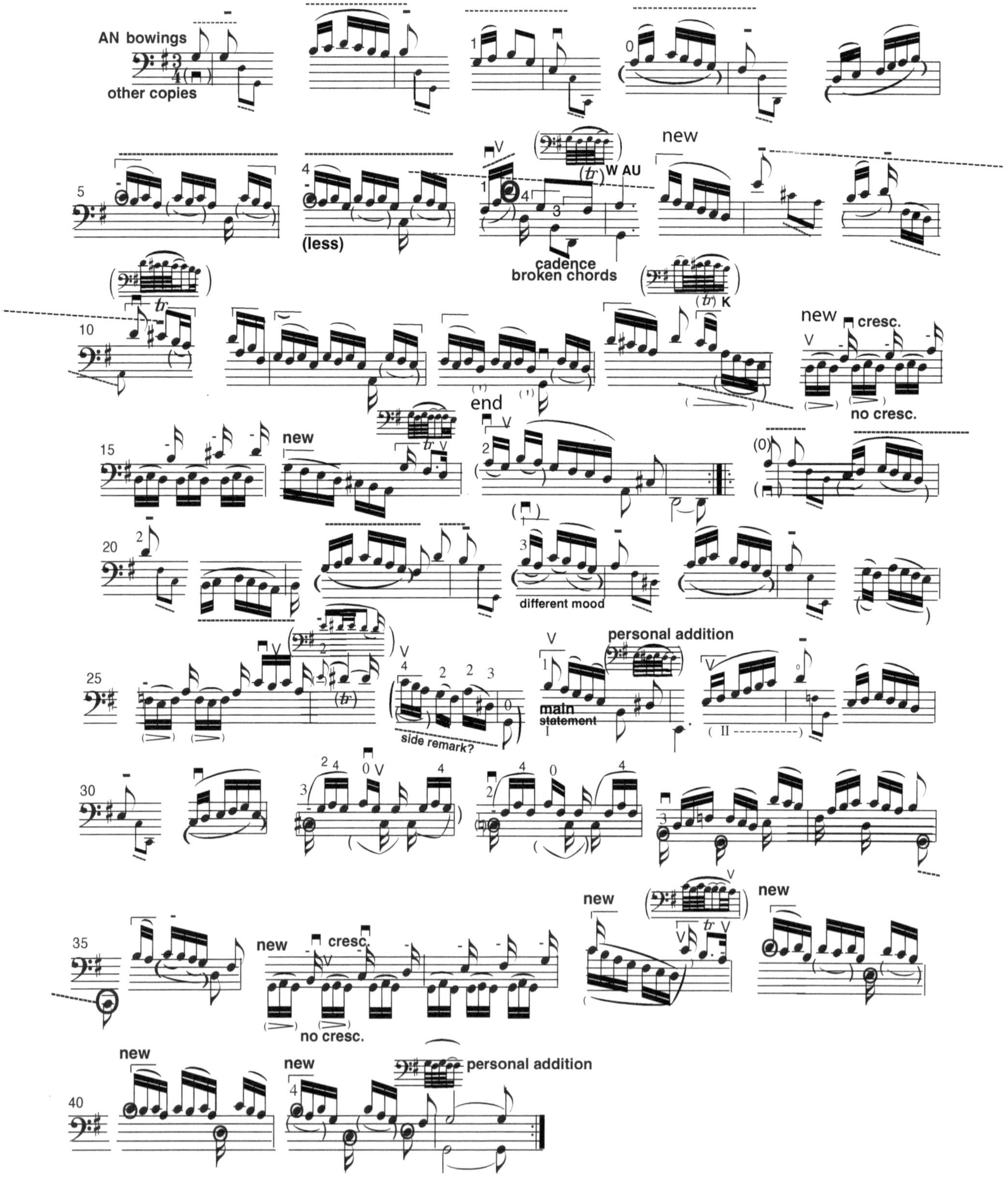

Sarabande
performance suggestion

Meter: Typical meter of a Sarabande is ♩ ♩ ♩   The 2nd beat is strengthened by tenser harmony or appogiaturas. The architectonic "building block" is two-bars unit.

Rhythm: Double-dotted rhythms are applied here in the alternative version.

Chords: Chords can be played 2+2 or 1+2 or 1+3 or be rolled (denoting melodic or bass lines).

Bowings: Bowings are according to AN. Bowings in brackets (other copies) can be used in the repeats.

Meter: Every bar has a meter of its own within an architectonic meter-unit of 2 bars sort of "active and passive".

Menuet I
performance suggestion

Here are two versions of the Menuets. The first suggests bowings according to An The other uses other copies' bowings. The choice is left to the player (to use them in the repeats or the Da-Capo). In both versions it is advisable to keep the inner meter of the individual bars (⌣ - -), the architectonic concept of two bars units and "active", "passive".

Menuet II performance suggestion

lighter? as if menuet II is solo (trio) in contrast to menuet I (tutti)
Architectonic meter-unit of two bars
(There is one ♭ at the key in all the copies. This
causes few uncertain cases of ♭ and ♮ like bar 3)

Menuet 1 Da capo

"Gigues must be played extremely fast"(Muffat 1653-1704). "Gigues is played with short and light bow strokes... there is a pulse beat on each bar"(Quantz 1697-1773).

In the 12 first bars Bach creates architectonically three groups

1	1	2	1	1	2	1	1	2
half bar	half bar	whole bar	half bar	half bar	whole bar	whole bar	whole bar	2 bars

Bars 9-12 are grouped as 2+2 bars. The same applies to the second part of the gigue.
Bowings are according to AN. Bowings in brackets are from the other copies.

Suite II

BMV 1008

PRELUDE
ALLEMANDE
COURANTE
SARABANDE
MENUET I – MENUET II
GIGUE

Prelude suite II remarks

This prelude is a masterful piece of architectonic design. An interval of a fifth, in the first bar, is enlarged into broken triad of a diminished seventh (bar 2) and then to an octave (bar 3). The prelude reaches its highest point in bars 40 and 42 when the interval of the fifth is now an octave and a fifth, repeated twice, a climax.

Moreover following the "horizon line" (see introduction page 14) we can see that the high e in bar 3 spans to the f in bar 20 and again an f in bar 29 and 36 and then to the g in bar 44 the climax of the movement, where the energy is the most intense.

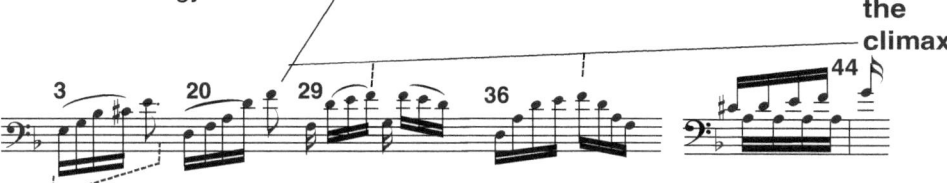

From there on everything calms down to the end.

Both the enlargements of the initial interval and the upscaling of the "horizon line" are an expression of the composer's development of his energy intensity.

Prelude suite II remarks — essence of harmonic and architectonic designs

There is a never-ending debate whether "arpeggiating" the chords was Bach's intention. Frederick Neumann writes " It is a mistake to transform those notes into arpeggiated figures... If, and only if, that last measure (before) had contained an obvious arpeggio formula, a case might be made...However, the melody in that last measure does not even resemble an arpeggio...(also) Bach...writes "arpeggio" or "arp" when he wants chords to be so treated... For these reasons it is quite certain that the chords were meant to be played as chords...The dotted half notes need not be held for their full value, but can be played with the kind of free rhythm, such as, say, dotted quarter notes (AU though marks see above). A player's decision .

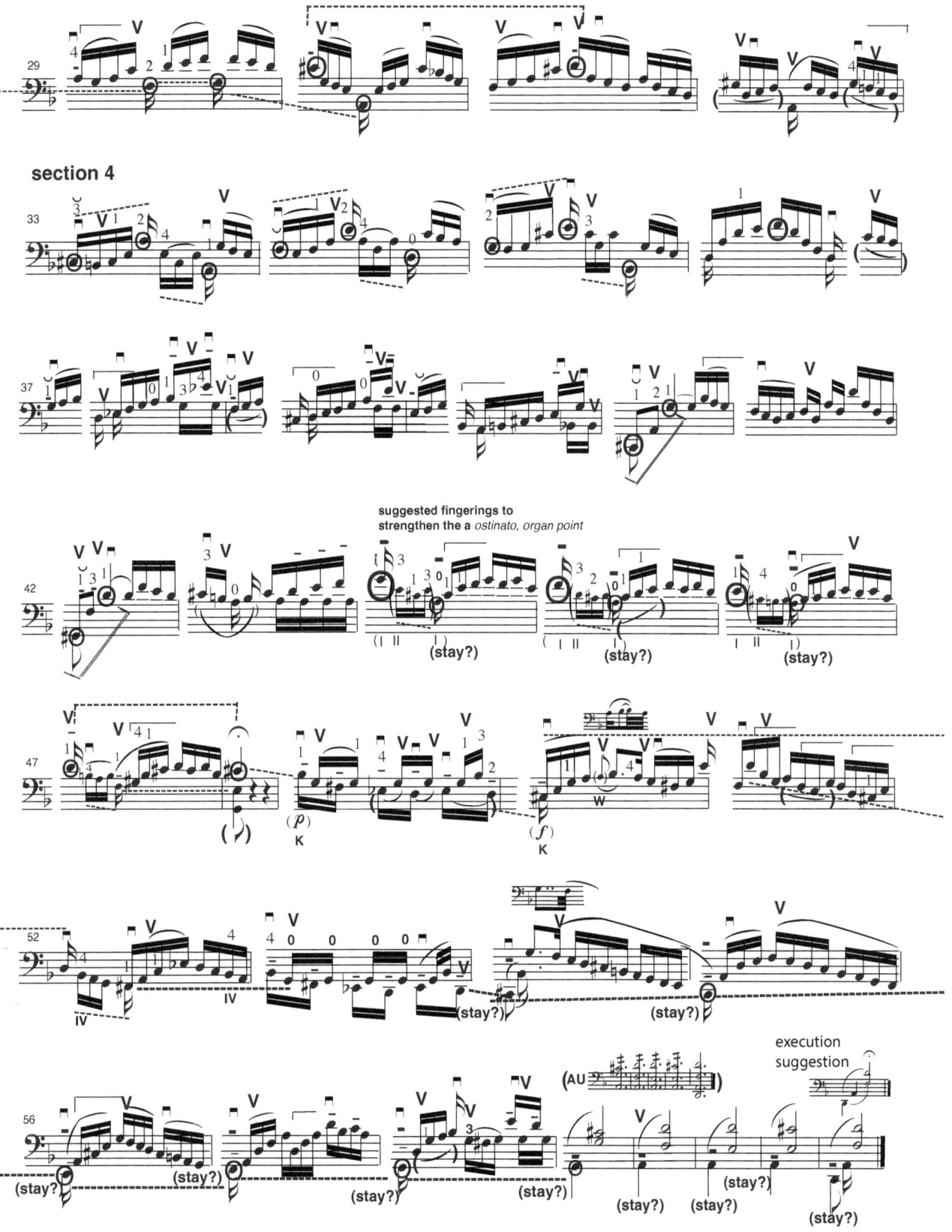

This moderately-fast allemande has a singing quality. Long units and syntax divisions are marked with dotted lines. Double-dotted rhythms were not written but were used in actual performances thus ♪♪ was played approximately as ♪..♪ but not automatically all the time. There was much flexibility in rhythmical expression. One can stay longer on the 1st notes of the tied two-notes' groups (marked -) and on the 1st notes of the four-notes' groups.

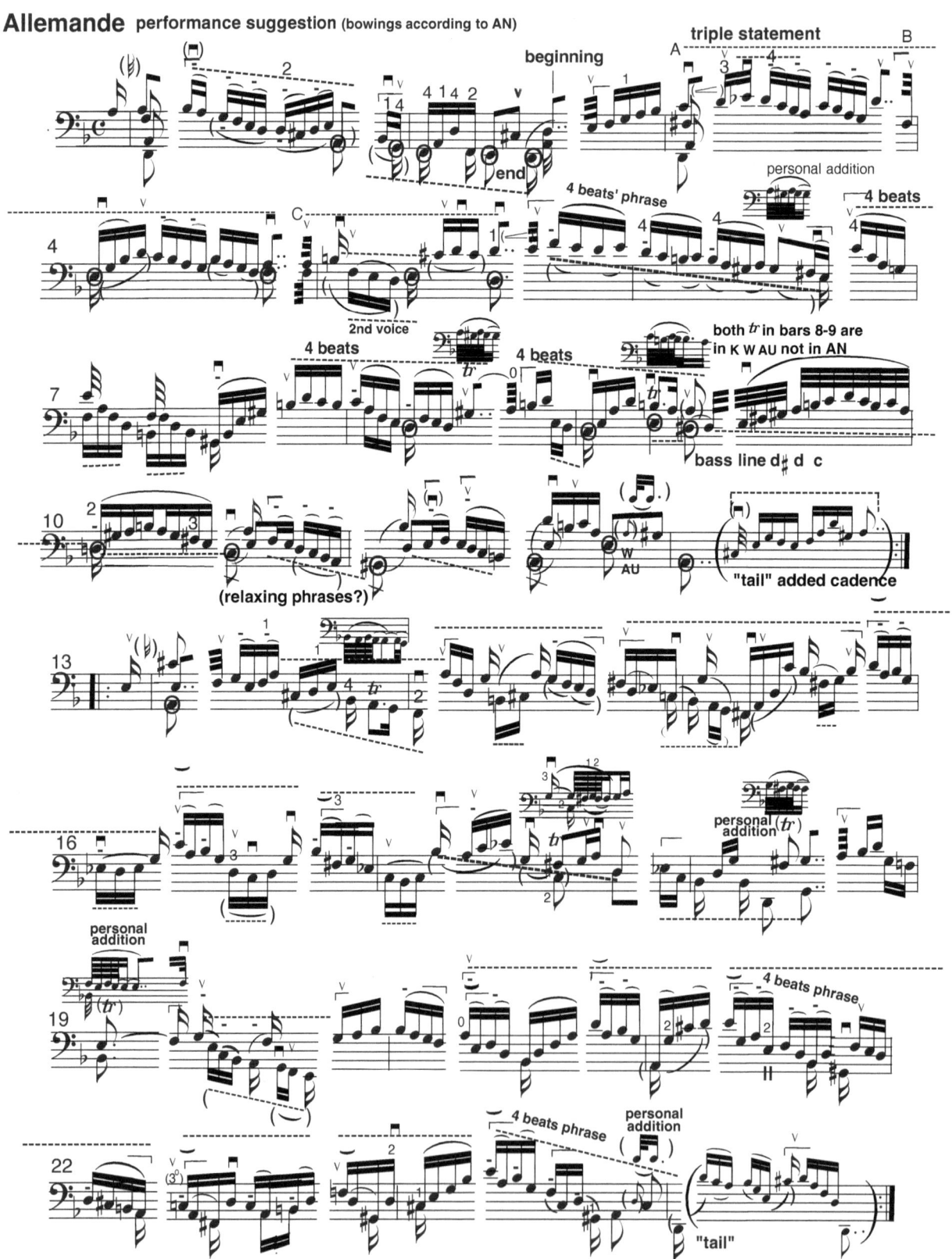

Courante performance suggestion

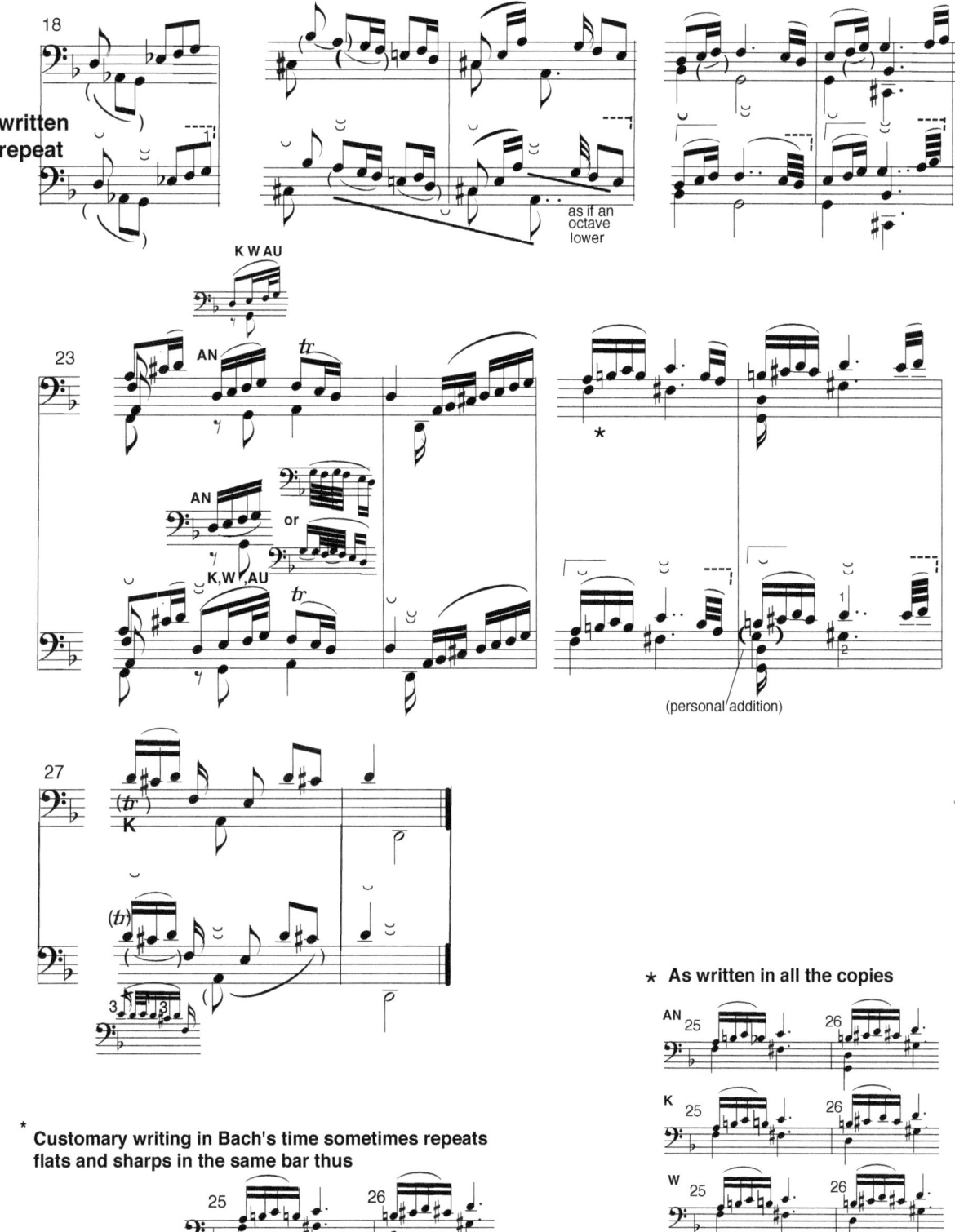

Suite III

BMV 1009

PRELUDE
ALLEMANDE
COURANTE
SARABANDE
BOURÉE I – BOURÉE II
GIGUE

Prelude 3rd Suite remarks

Bach wrote his Cantata no.68 in 1725 (probably few years after the 3rd suite). In the 2nd movement, aria, for a singer and a violoncello piccolo obligato. The violoncello obligato part is full of similar passages to those in the prelude of the 3rd suite. In the middle part of this aria when the singer declares "Jesus ist da" (Jesus is here) the cello piccolo plays the opening phrase of the prelude:

There are two things to pay attention

1) Tempo: the aria is titled presto. Kellner in his copy added presto to the title prelude.

2) Meter: The aria is written in $\frac{4}{4}$. If we look closer at the prelude we can speculate (as far as meter is concerned) that Bach could have written the beginning of this prelude like this:

Bach may have thought like that but he wrote (probably as was customary):

The prelude is in $\frac{3}{4}$.
A meter starts on the 2nd beat of the 2nd bar. It will eventually change in bar 19 (C.P.E.Bach" meter must be changed in order to arouse") .
Meter does not necessarily follow the barlines (C.P.E Bach "common time is indicated but not prescribed to the entire piece").

J.S Bach: Six Suites for Cello Solo BMV 1007-1012

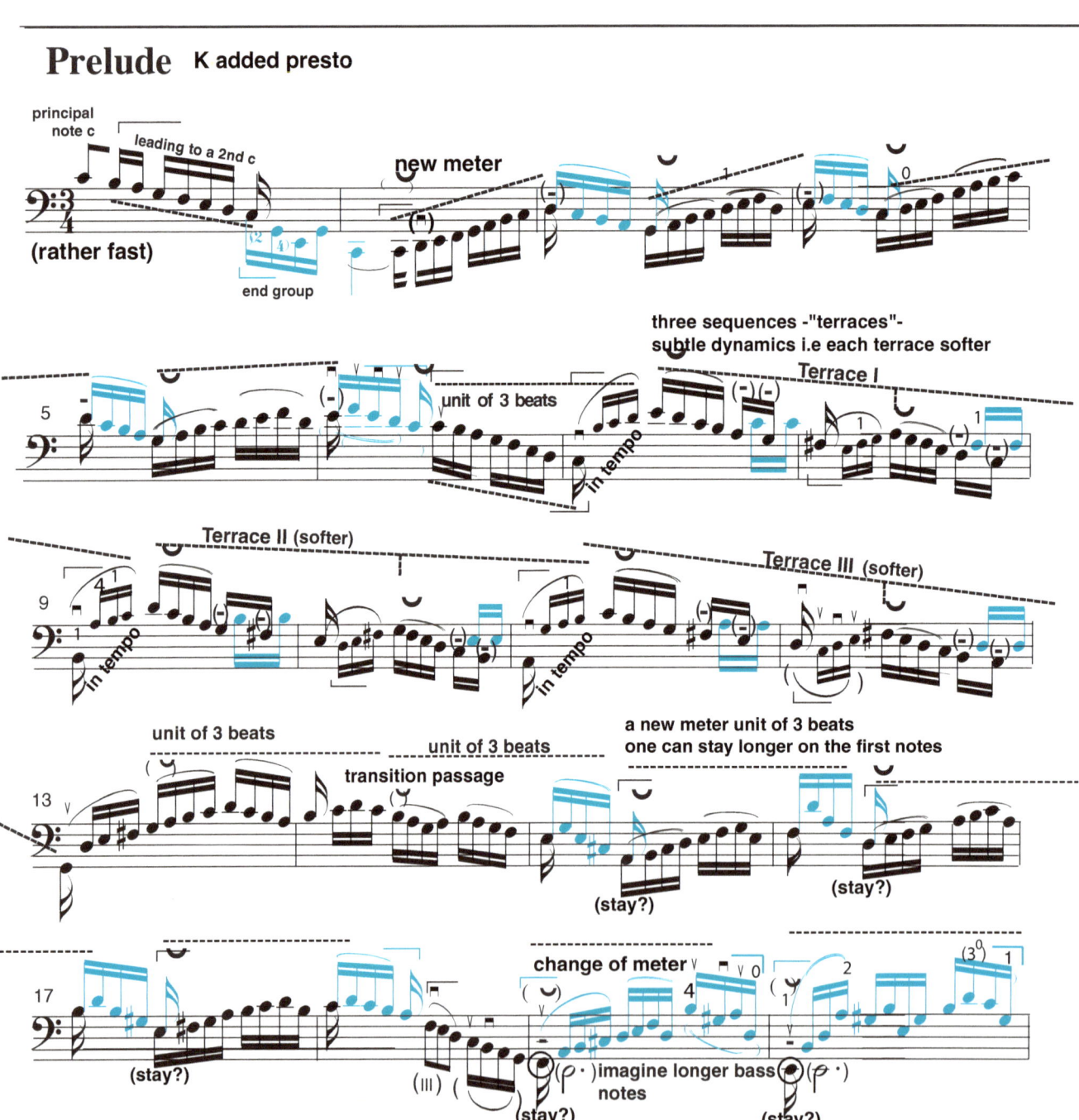

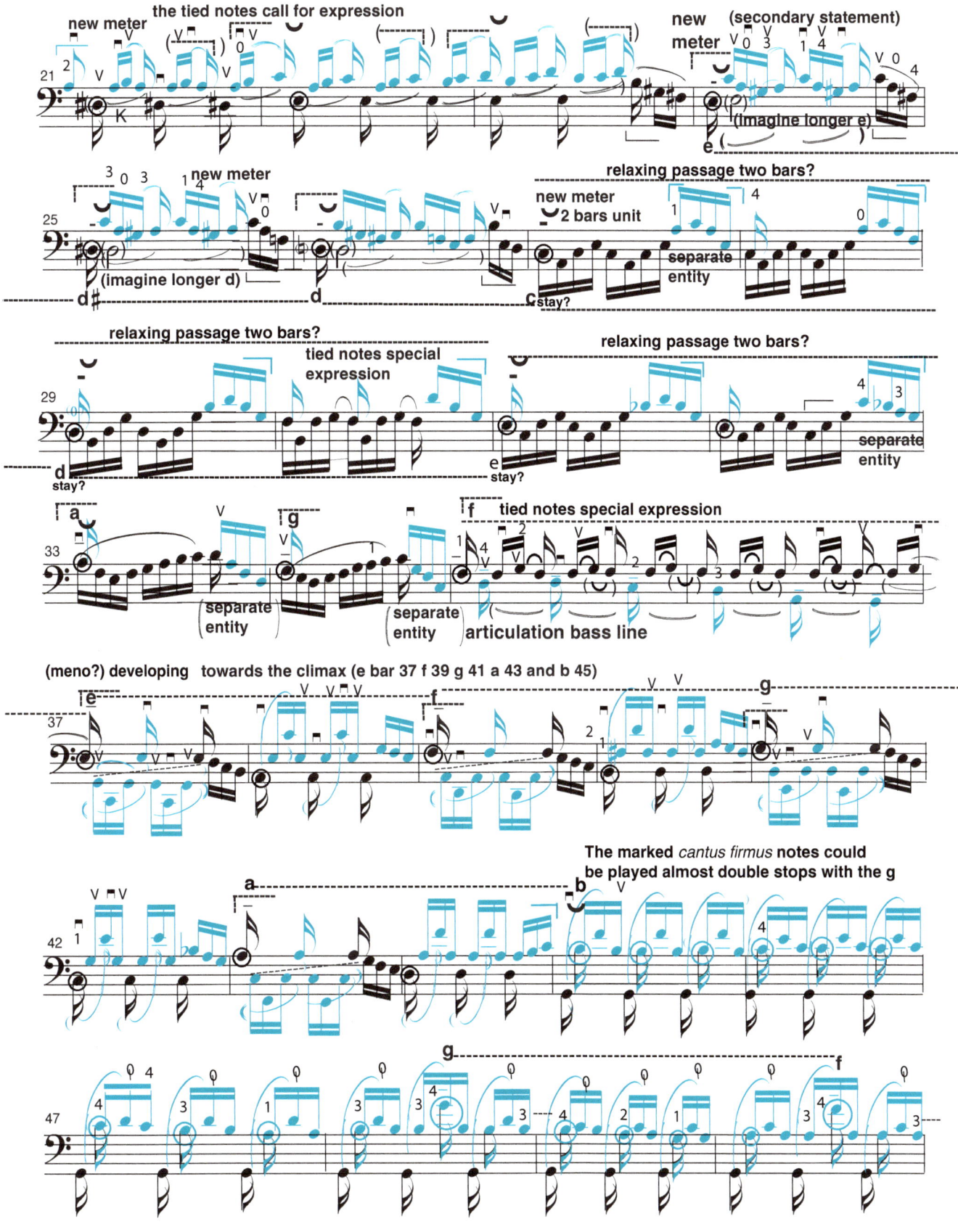

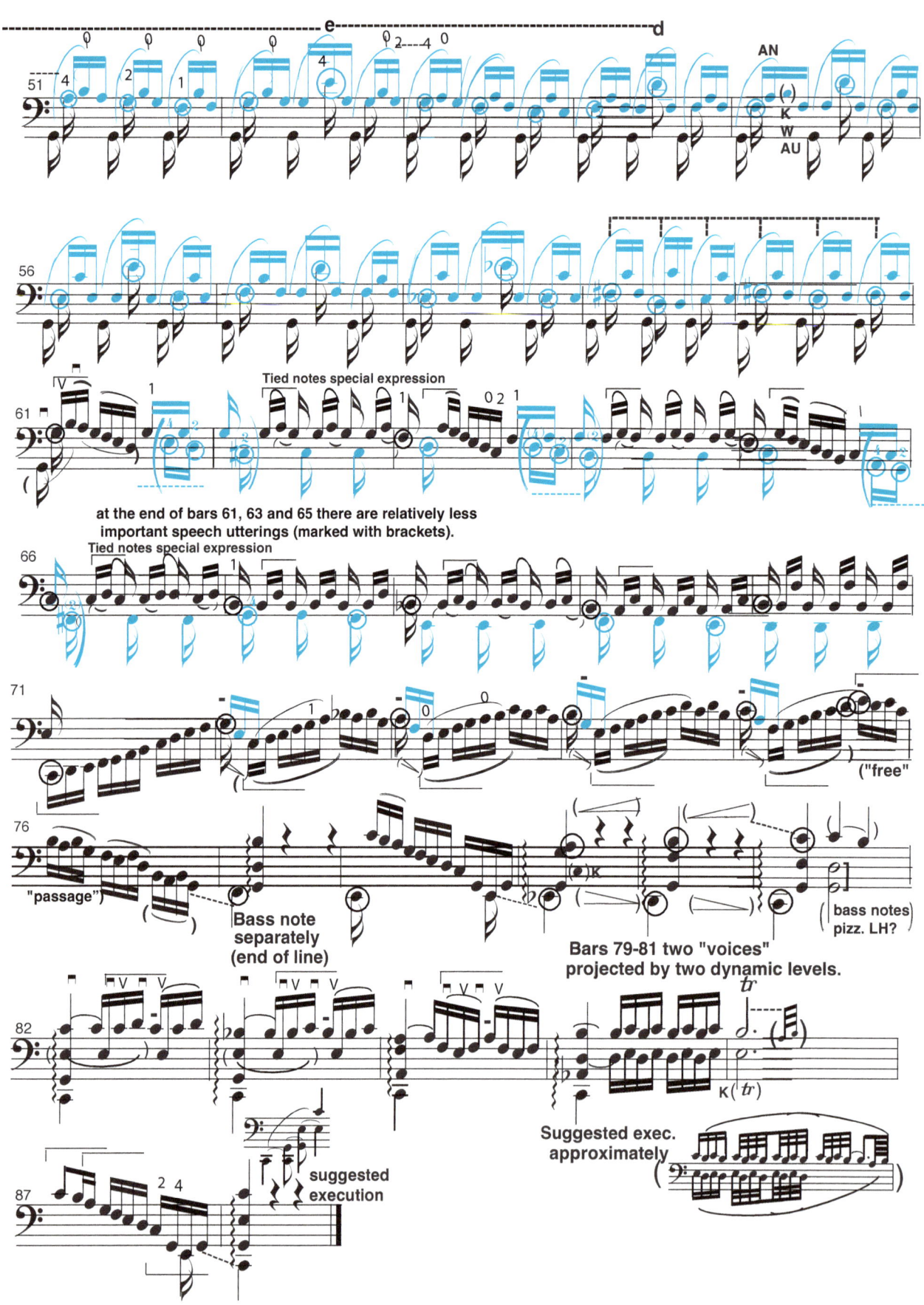

"Allemande is a serious and dignified movement and should be so performed" (J.G. Walther 1732)
Some rhythmical patterns prompt performers to play this particular allemande as a strong-accented fast dance movement, disregarding the fact that allemande is a movement with rhetoric quality, like the air, with a moderate tempo and an inner singing quality.
Meter does not necessarily follow the barlines (see introduction Meter) i.e. a new meter starts on the 4th beat of bar 2. *
The pale-shaded (blue) notes denote the "lighter" side of a two-beats' meter (see introduction page 5).

Allemande performance suggestion

* Variations of meter can be found in the amazing irregular statement of 7 beats in the beginning (8 if we include the upbeat). It is up to the player to find his own interpretation and his choice of the meter. Here are some possible examples:

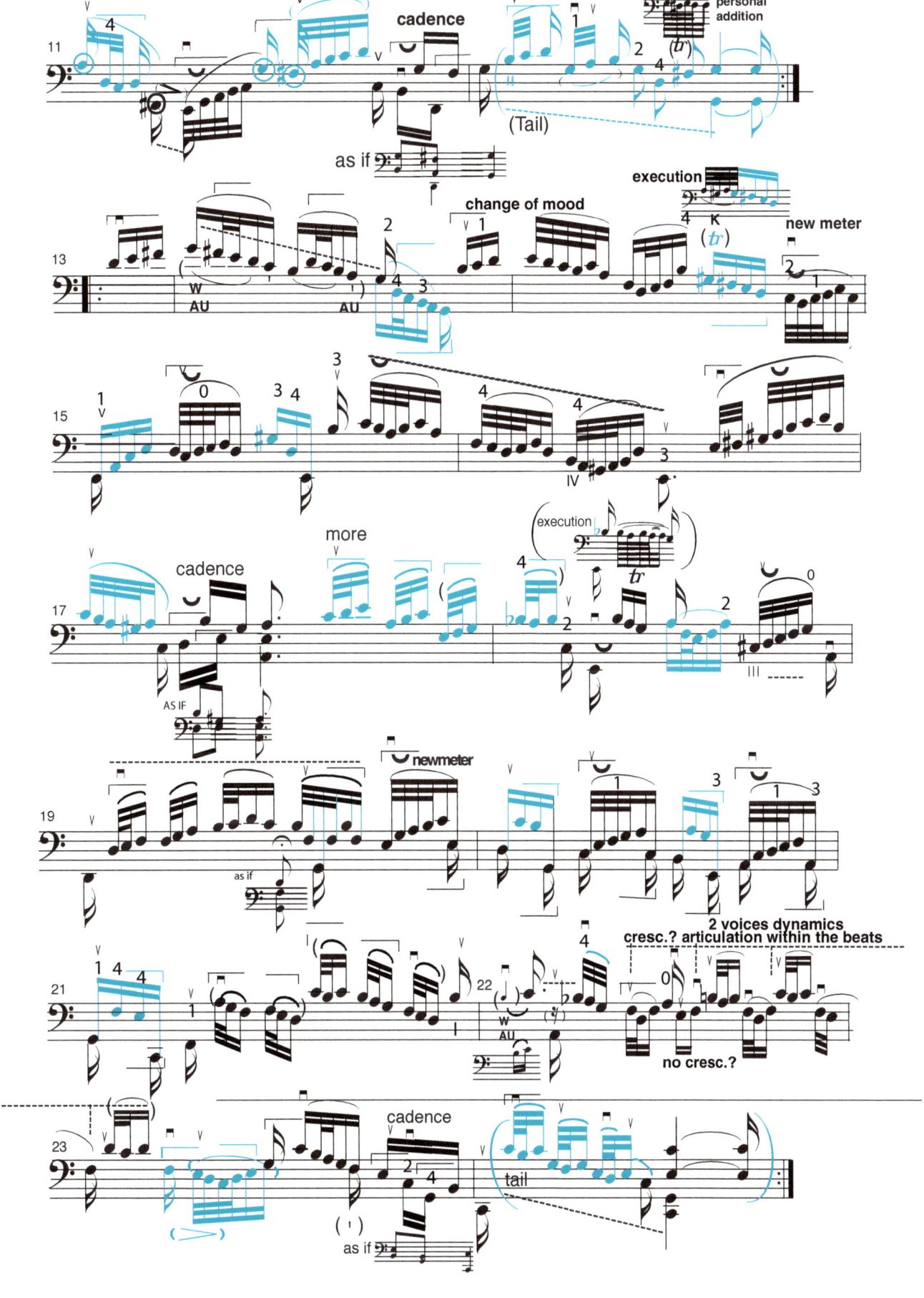

The meter in this moderately fast courante (like the ones in the 1st, 4th and the 6th suites) is a unit of two-bars, an "active" 1st bar and "passive" 2nd one (Kirnberger who studied with Bach : "there are melodies... that entire measures are alternately heavy and light so that...an entire measure consist(s) of one beat...then two measures set together to make a single one"). The inner breathing of the courant's organism is:

Bach chose his rhythmical pulse thoughtfully and wrote this courante in ♩ notes and not in ♪ notes.

Some players tend to play this courante very fast and it sounds as if it was written

It might not be what Bach had in mind.

Courante performance suggestion

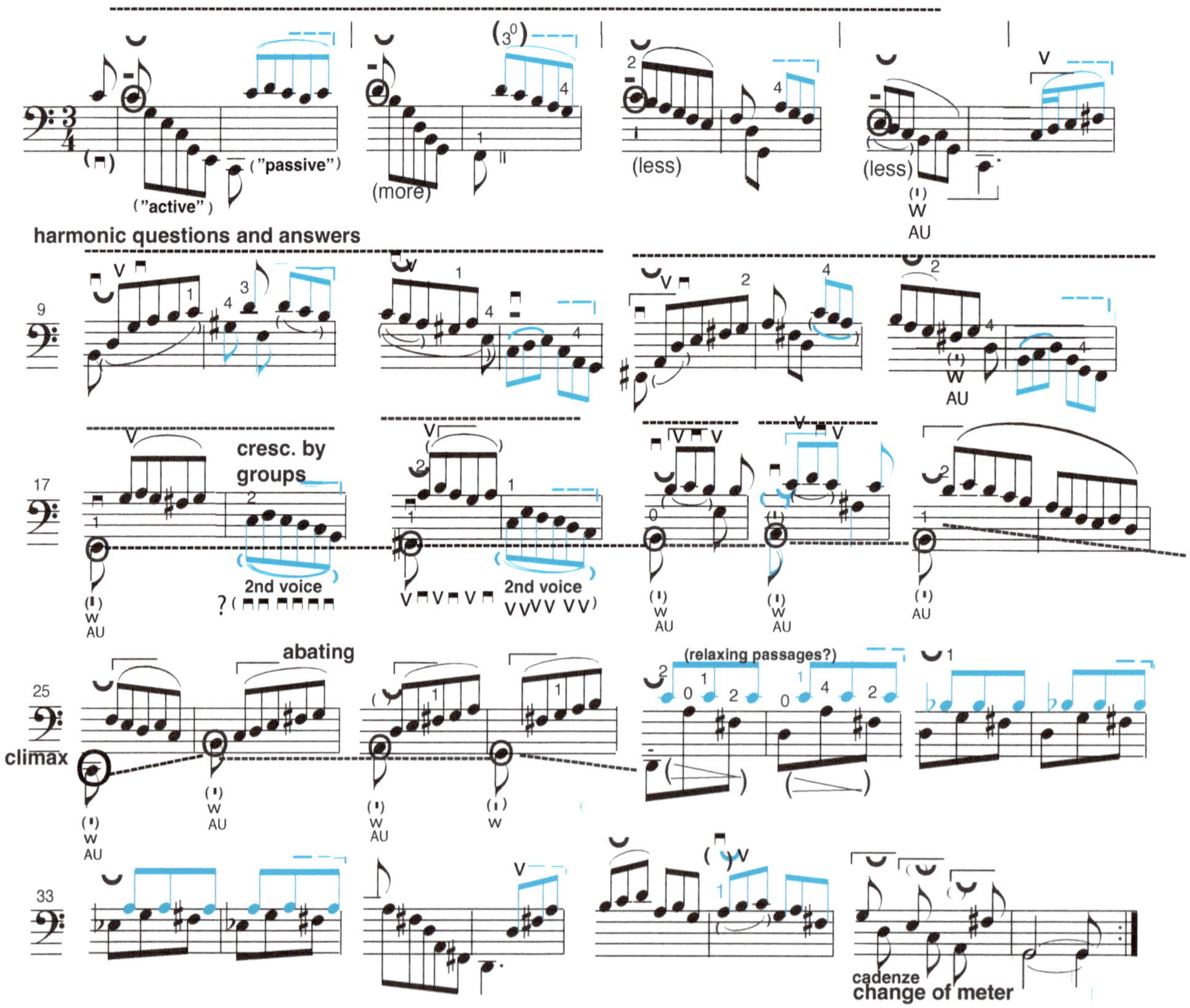

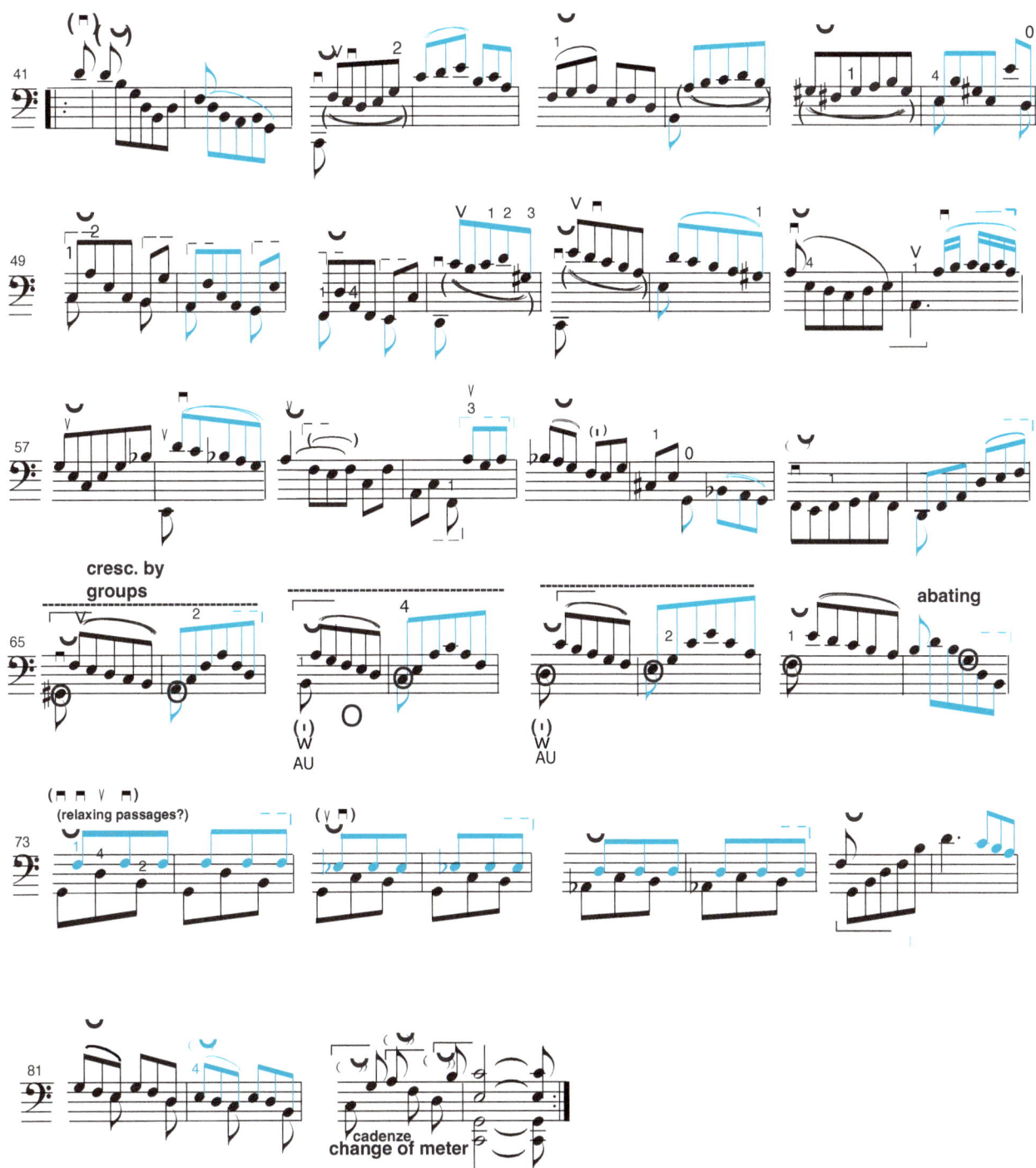

SARABANDE performance suggestion

Meter: heavy, heavier, relax — architectonic unit 2 bars

Bach's writing stresses the meter by a tenser harmony on the 2nd beat (i.e. bars 1, 2, 3).
It is suggested to absorb this meter in every bar to create a special sarabande's chracter.
Bowings are according to AN. In the suggested written repeat there are embellishments from other copies.
Architectonically Bach uses the scheme of 1 bar, 1 bar, 2 bars

Written repeat

personal addition

"A pulse beat falls on each bar" (Quantz). The meter which is a two-bars unit helps to break the "routine" accent on each bar.

The 2 voices are denoted here by the 2 print shades:

Bourée I performance suggestion

The title in K is Boure et alternat

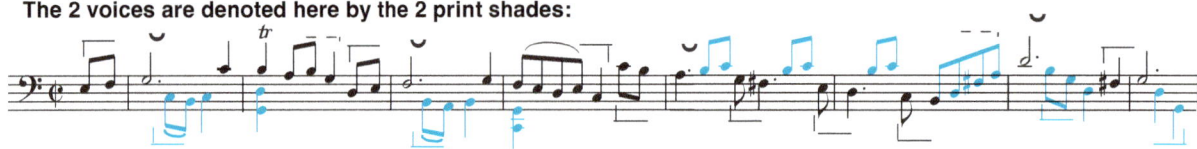

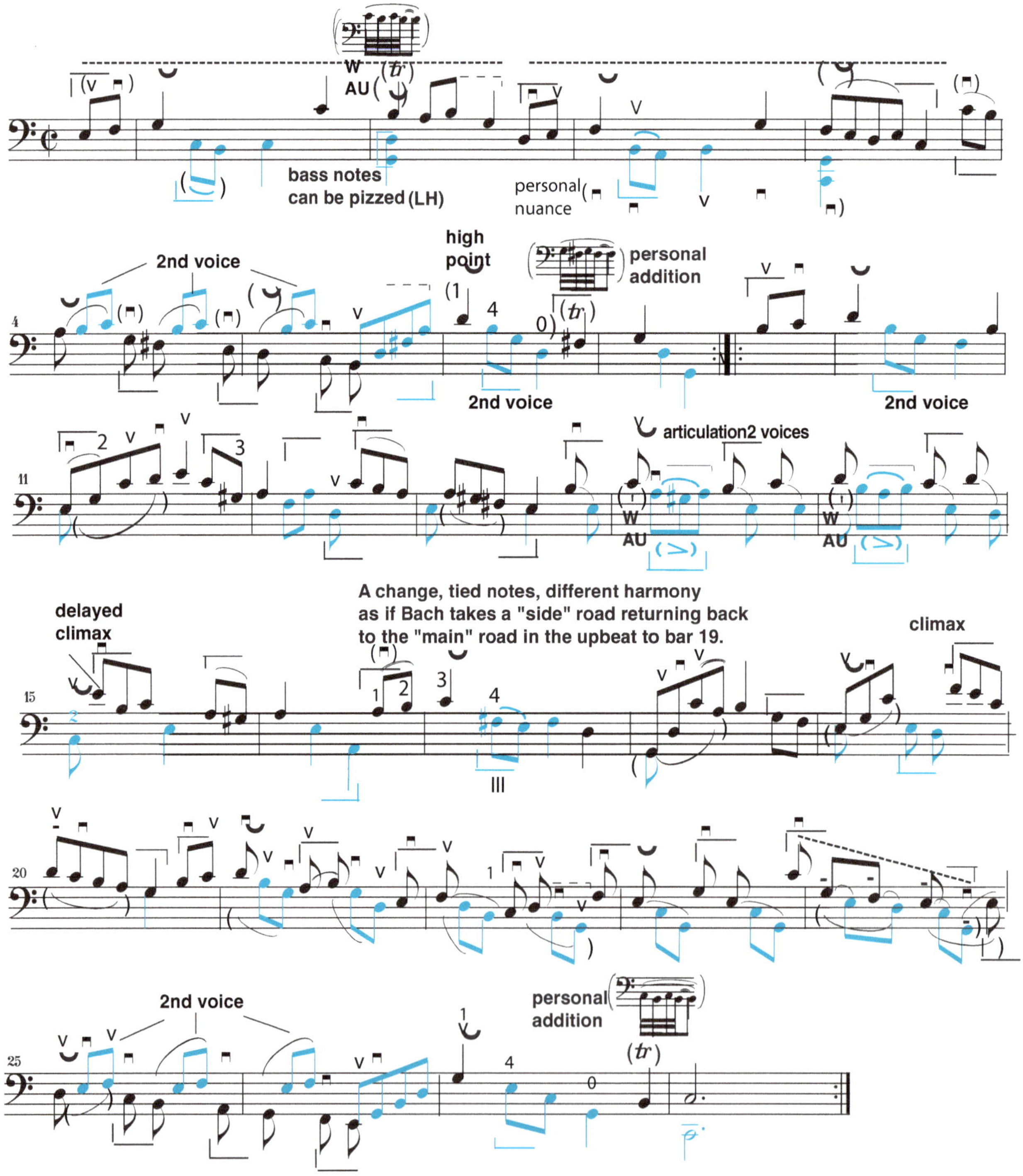

In bouree II the meter is a two-bars unit. There is a difference between the relatively "more important statements" and the relatively secondary ones - the ornamental connective lines (marked by the blue paler print). The essence of bouree II can be simplified like this:

In Kellner's copy this bouree is titled "Boure 2 pian". It is suggested to play bouree II mainly on the d string like a solo "trio" and pian(o) in contrast to the "tutti" of the bouree I.

Bourée II performance suggestion

In all the copies there are were only two ♭ near the key signature. The editor added more ♮ and ♭ in the text to avoid misunderstandings. K put ♭ at the end of bar 4.

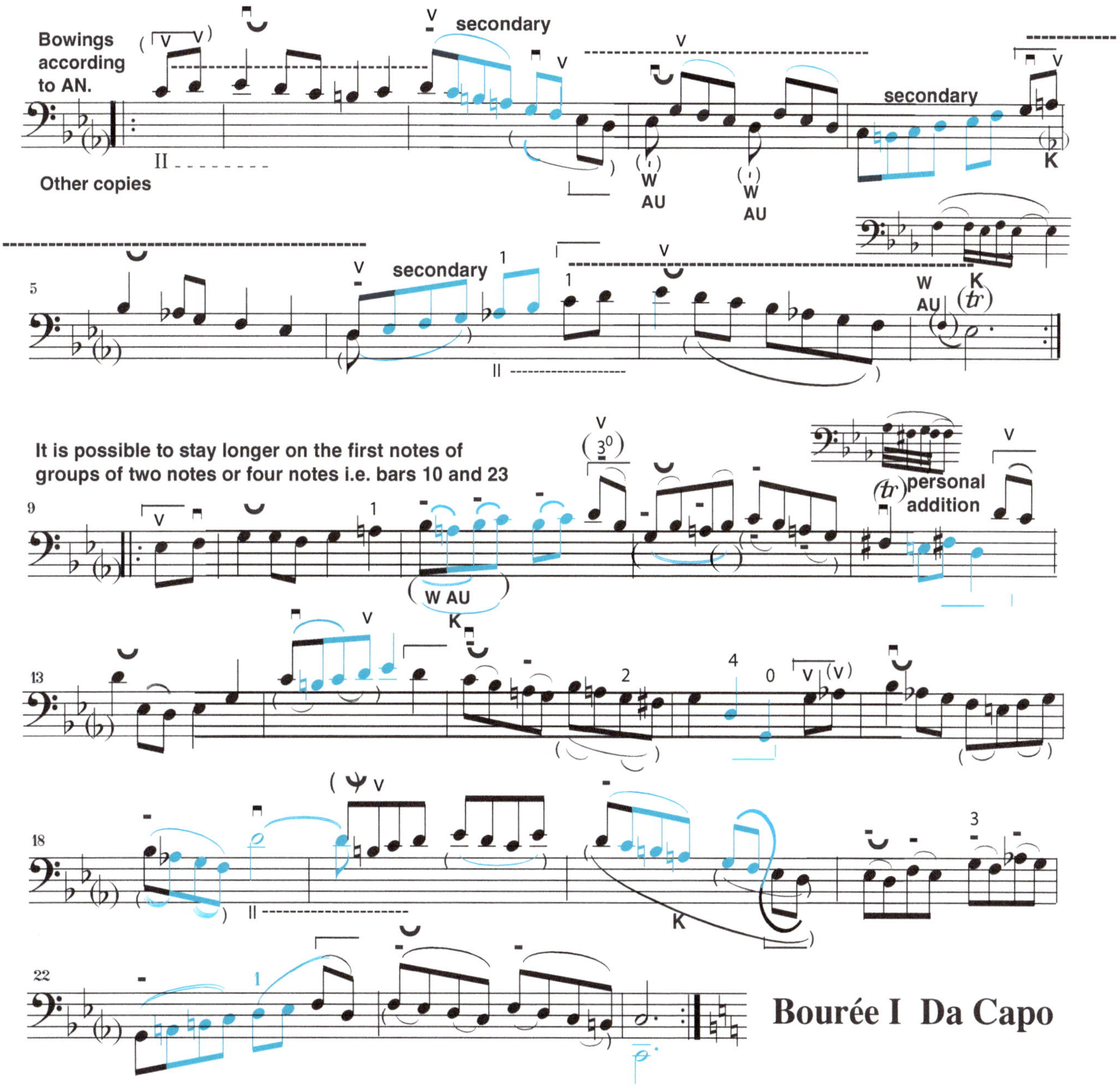

It is possible to stay longer on the first notes of groups of two notes or four notes i.e. bars 10 and 23

Bourée I Da Capo

"Gigues must be played extremely fast" "Gigue is played with short and light bow strokes. There is a pulse beat on each bar" (Quantz 1697-1773). Meter is based on two-bar units and there is a four-bars-phrase-units as longer statements. The pale shaded (blue) notes denote a second voice. Different bow speeds can articulate different voices which can also be played on different strings.

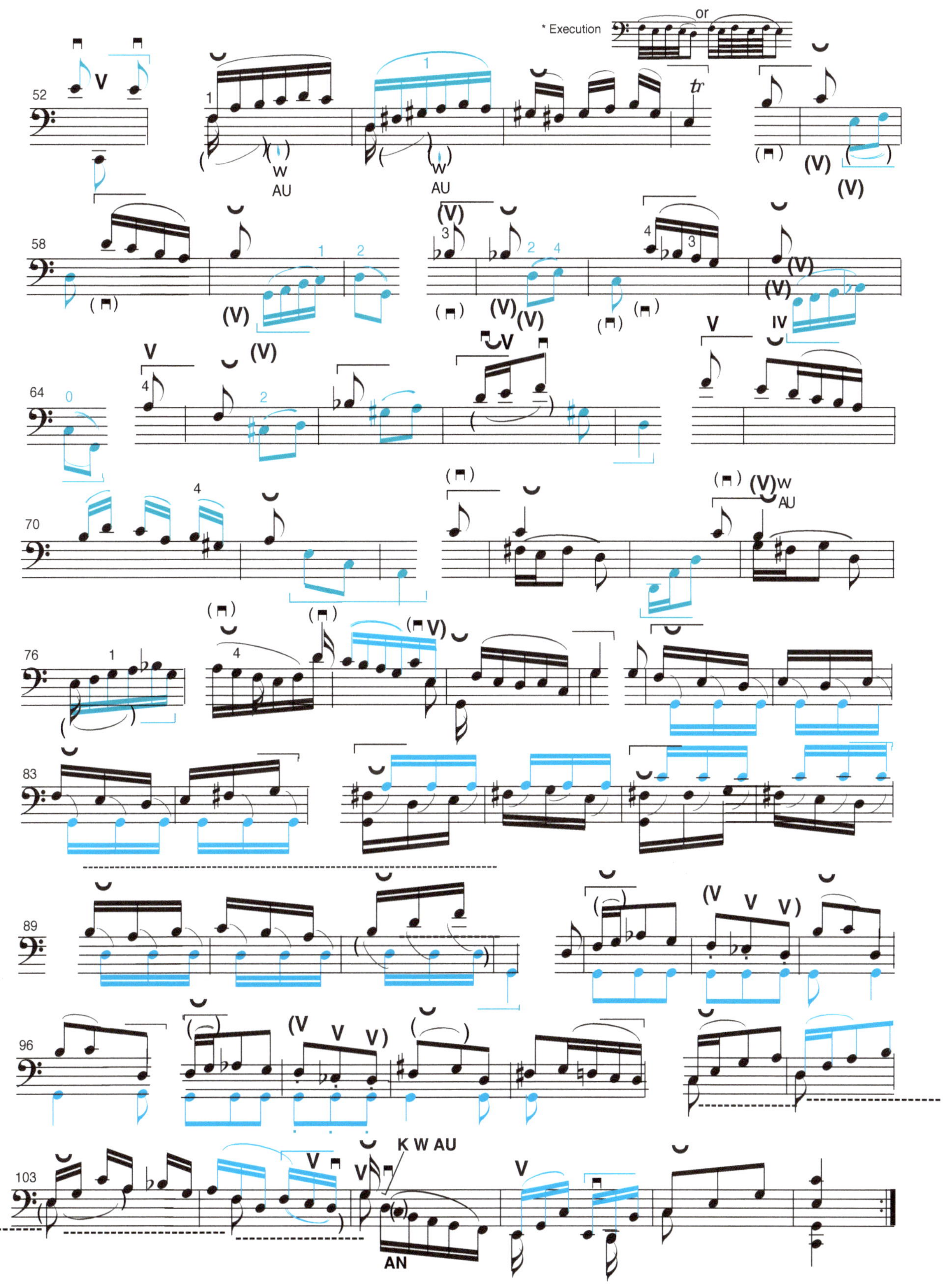
* Execution
or
52
W
AU
W
AU
58
64
70
W
AU
76
83
89
96
103
K W AU
AN

Suite IV

BMV 1010

PRELUDE
ALLEMANDE
COURANTE
SARABANDE
BOURÉE I – BOURÉE II
GIGUE

Prelude (AN Preludium)
performance suggestion
dual statements unit 2 bars articulation
1st "weighty" main notes only in 1st bar of a unit

Suggested bowings to help articulate the dual statements.
Suggested fingerings to help harmonic intonation (double-stop positions).
Meter starts on the 1st beat. Phrasing starts on the 2nd note.
Articulation within the pulse beats.

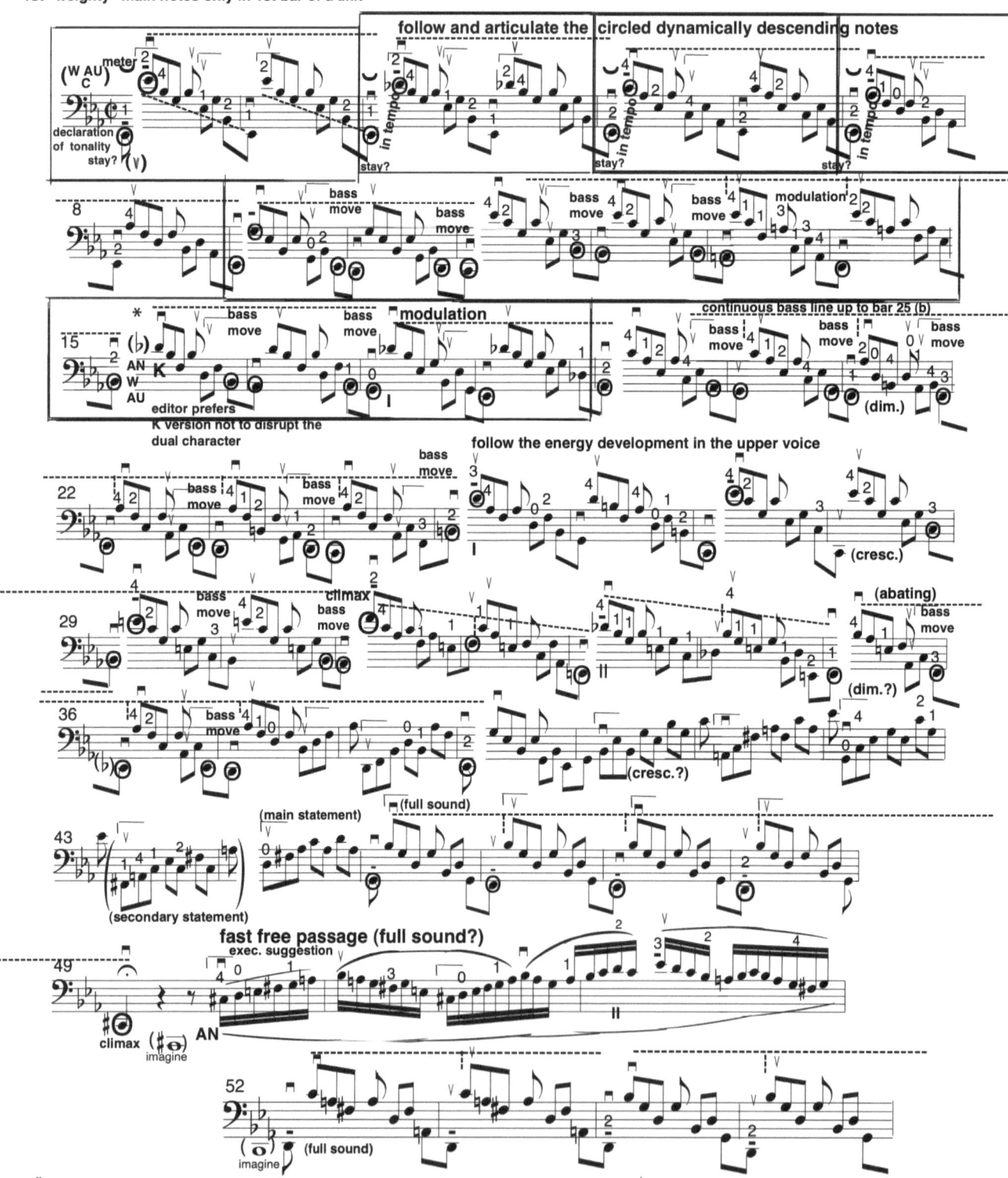

*We shall never know the true facts about mistakes and their sources. The ♭ in the 2nd note of bar 16 appears in 3 copies (K does not have it). In these 3 copies there is no ♭ in the lower d (the usual way of writing). Owing to this and because of the overall <u>dual</u> character of this prelude it looks as if the ♭ in bar 16 was a mistake (one bar too soon?!) in one source which was copied by the others. It makes musical sense if bars 15-16 are with the same upper notes as one unit like the rest of the prelude.

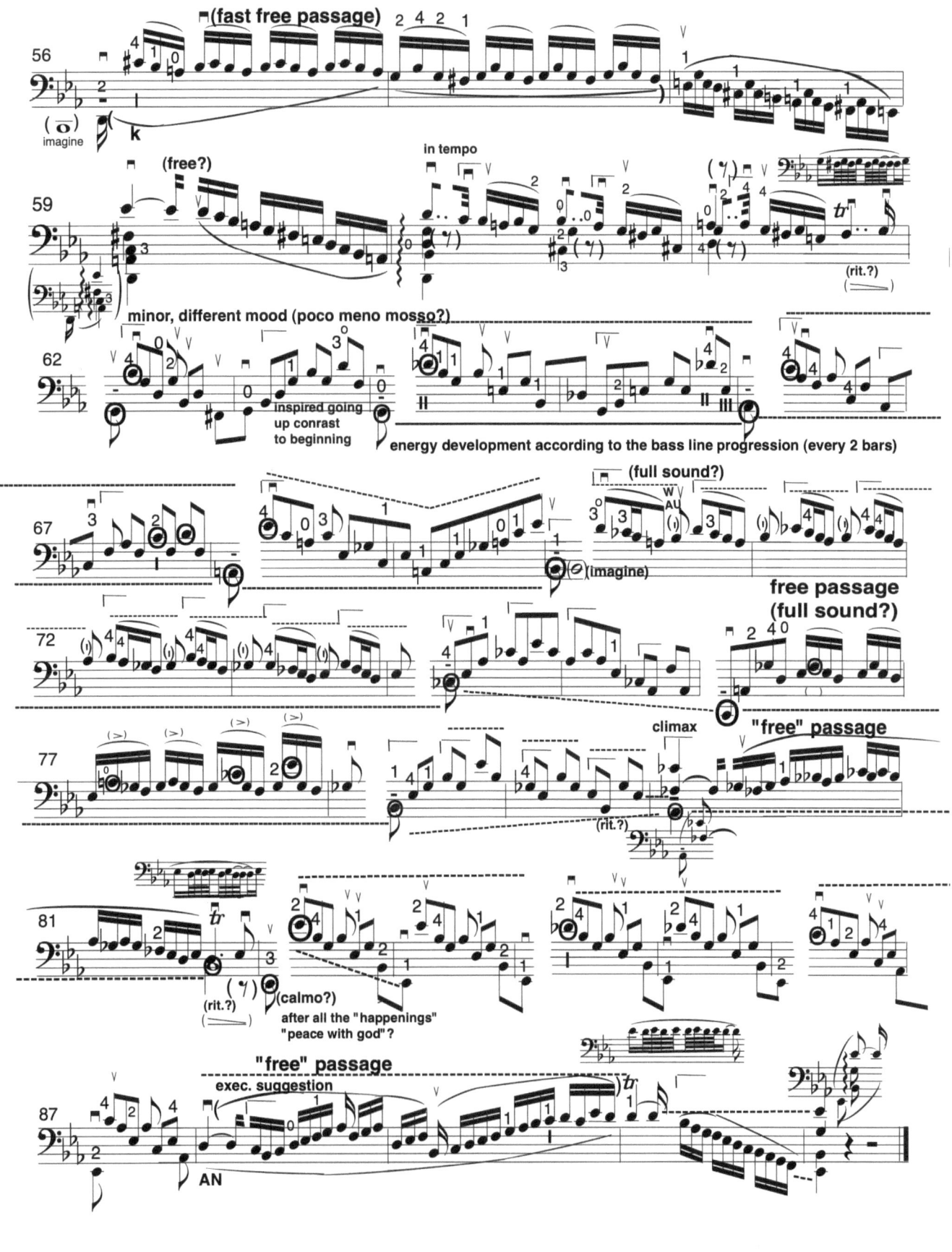

The suggested meter is

This meter (half bars, in two?) helps to decide the tempo.
The syntax is masterly constructed. The last notes of the phrases are also the first notes of the next ones:

merging

In the finer articulation,
when merging, the first note of every group is relaxing softer
dynamically, but it is also an onset of a new energy.

Here is a chart showing Bach's two-dimentional writing and development of energy tides in bars 7-12. climax
The same in bars 31-34. upper voice

climax
lower voice

Energy develops with upper line f (bar 7) - g (bar 8) - a b c d e f (bars 9-11) and the g (bar 11) as a climax. But there is also the line of the lower voice
b♭ (bar 7)- c (bar 8) - d e♭ f g a♭ (bars 9-11). The b♭ in bar 11 is a sort of a "delayed climax" (after the upper voice g). This kind of a delayed climax
in another voice is often used by Bach in his suites.

ALLEMANDE

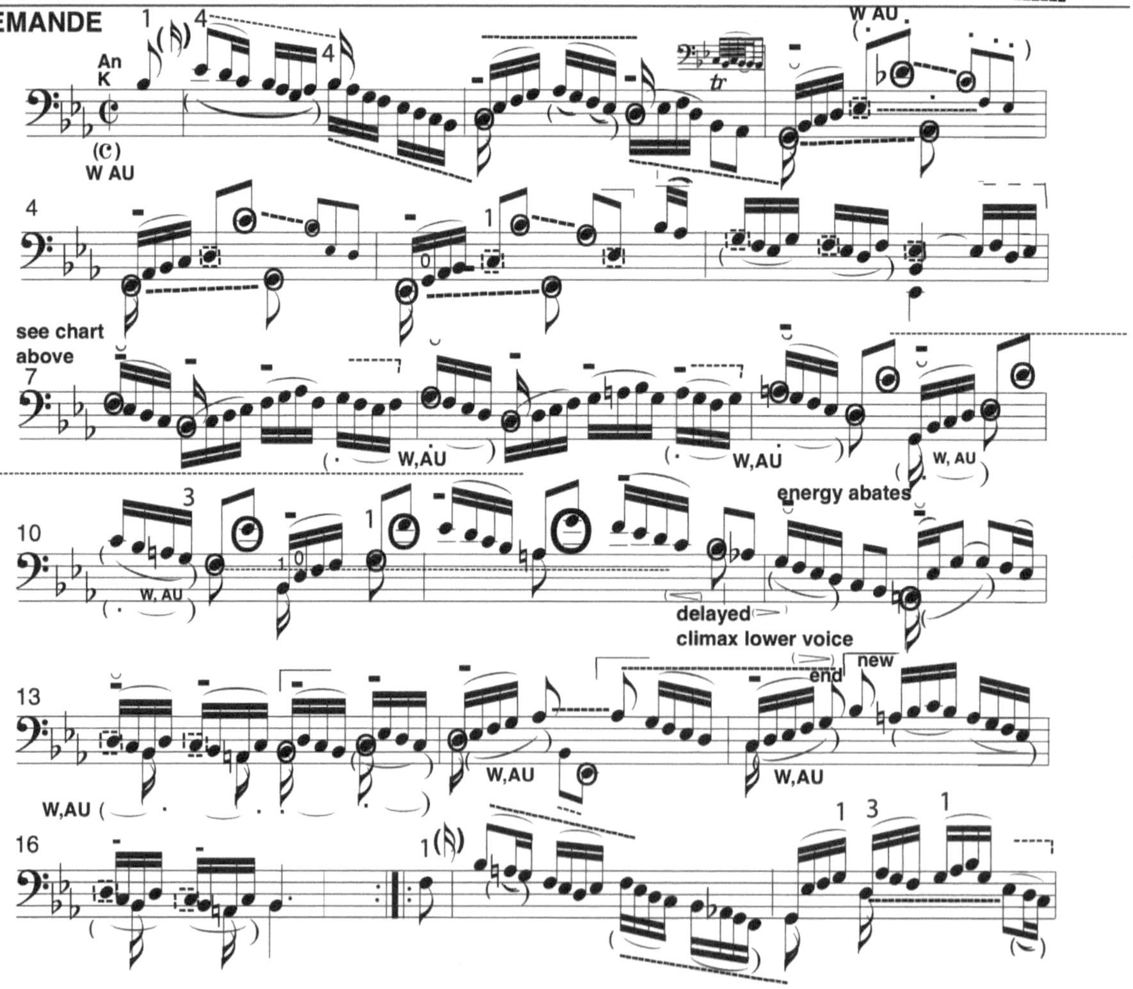

Rhythmic inequality in length and volume was used in the first note of a group of two, also of a group of four. It may be held longer. One may use this inequality in bars 23 and 24 and in similar places.

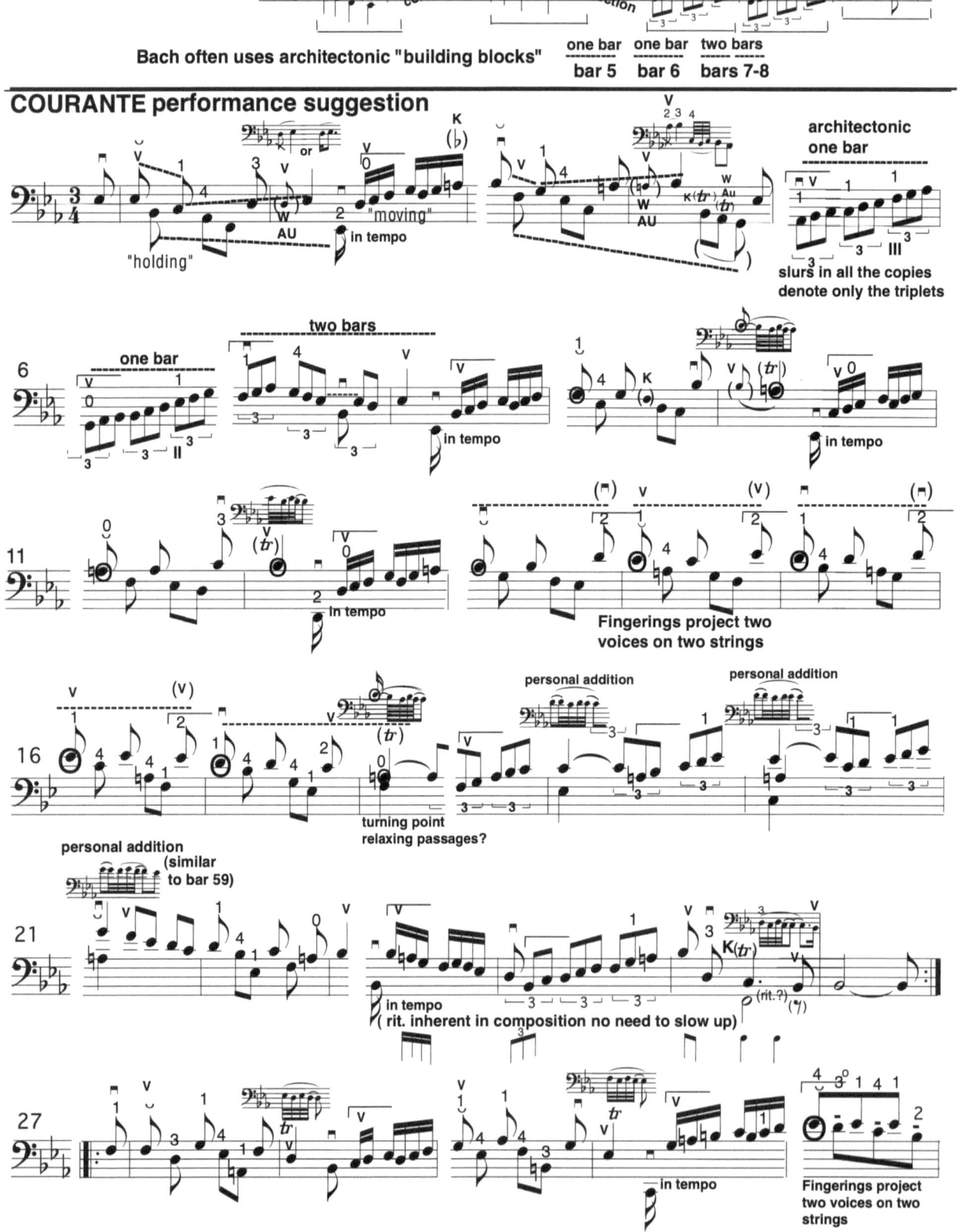

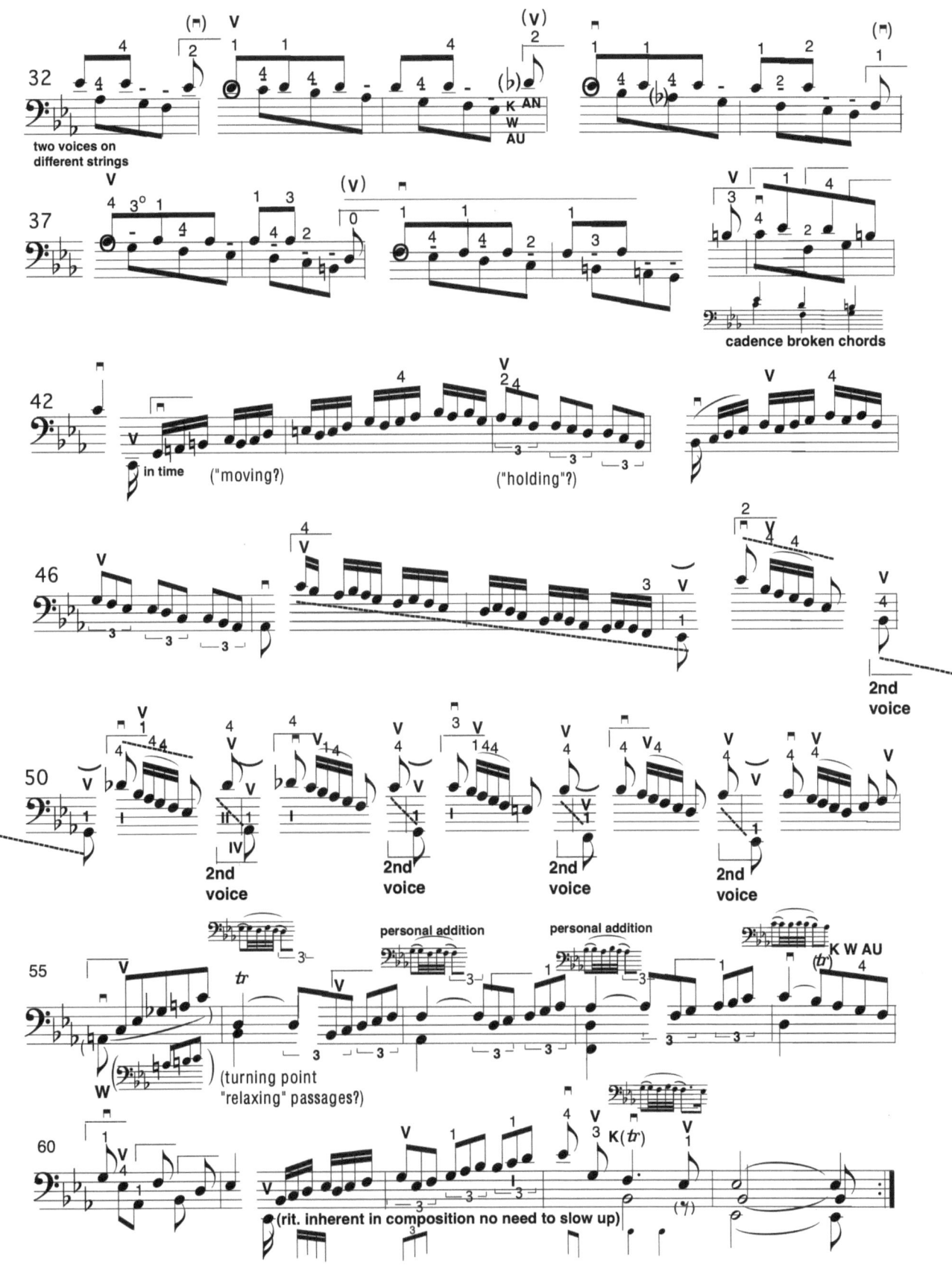

Sarabande architectonic outlook

In this extraordinary unique sarabande Bach the innovator deviates from the usual form.

There are 2 groups of 2 bars'-units

an irregular group of 3 bars building up intensity and only 1 bar abating (everything in perfect balance of form!)

closing the 1st part with a group of 4 bars (1+1+2).

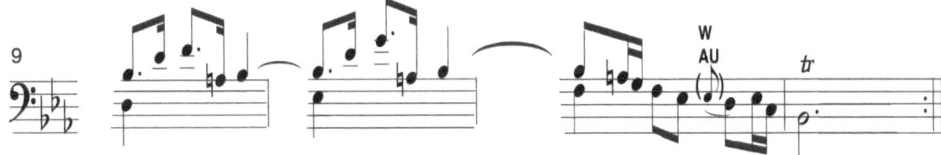

In the 2nd part there are 4 groups of 2 bars

again an irregular group of 4 bars (1+3)

a group of 4 bars (1+1+2)   Bach could have finished by skipping bars 27-30 going directly to bar 31 like in the 1st part. He chose to create a special harmonic intensification for 4 bars (27-31).

closing with 2 groups of 2 bars   climax

The meter  is inhered in each bar of the two-bars' unit.
heavy heavier relax.

The melodic line, in this two-bars' unit, is "accompanied" by chords with sustained appogiaturas. The harmonic solutions come only on the second beats of the 2nd bars of a units.

The 3rd beat of a 1st bar of a unit is almost always tied (legato) to the 1st beat of the 2nd bar. The tied legato signs are missing only in bars 1-2 (except k) and bars 3-4, but they exist throughout in all the copies or in some of them or in one of them. To repeat the same note in the upper voice with a chord sounds is disturbing musically. It is suggested to keep consistently the tied slur to the 1st beat and give this sarabande a special character.

When it is impossible to play the melody and the chord together the performer could play only the bass notes imagining the upper voice.

Sarabande performance suggestion

Suggested meter

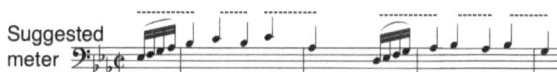

Bouree I performance suggestion

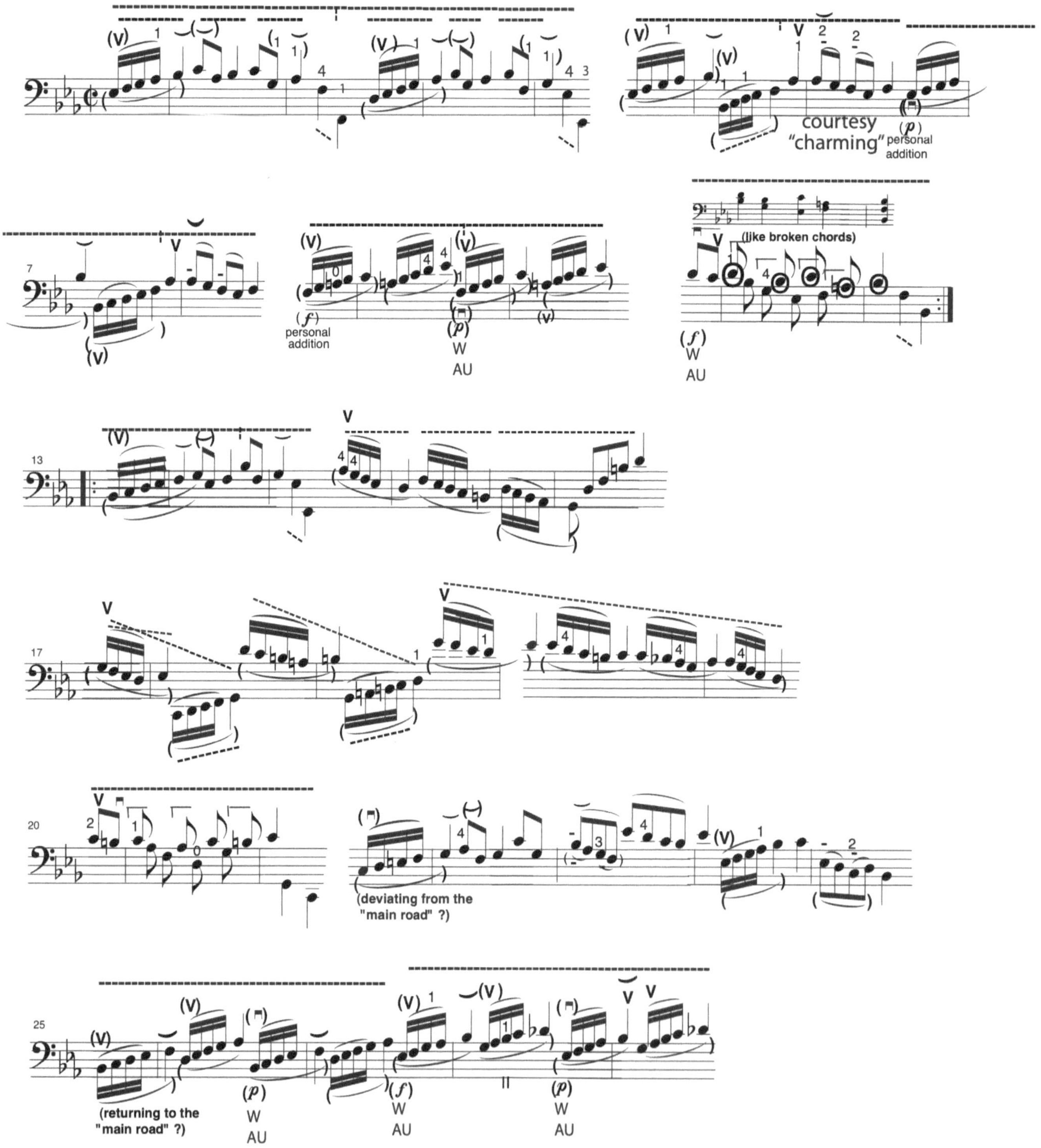

Playing the first note of each group of three notes throughout the gigue will help to absorb the tides' energy, the tension and relaxation and the harmonic "questions and answers".

Suite V

BMV 1011

PRELUDE
ALLEMANDE
COURANTE
SARABANDE
GAVOTTE I – GAVOTTE II
GIGUE

First version - Scordatura
Second version - Normal tuning performance suggestion
Third version - Adaptation of the lute Ms. for cello

The issues of baroque cello versus "modern" one and scordatura versus normal tuning are a matter of personal conviction. One can always find a suitable kind of sound in a normal tuning to fit a personal conception of Bach's sound and style.

The rendering of the text depends on articulation, phrasing, meter, tempo and many other elements, which are introduced here.

Allemande
(Scordatura)

Allemande has a cantilena character. The copies are not consistant in their bowings. In the lute version Bach himself wrote out the applications of rhythms in performance. They are marked here in the text. Everything is flexible and the applications are to be executed approximately and not automatically everytime. It is left to the taste and logic of the player to fit everything to the musical contents. The bowings of the fast notes are optional. One can stay longer on the 1st notes of groups of tied two or four notes.

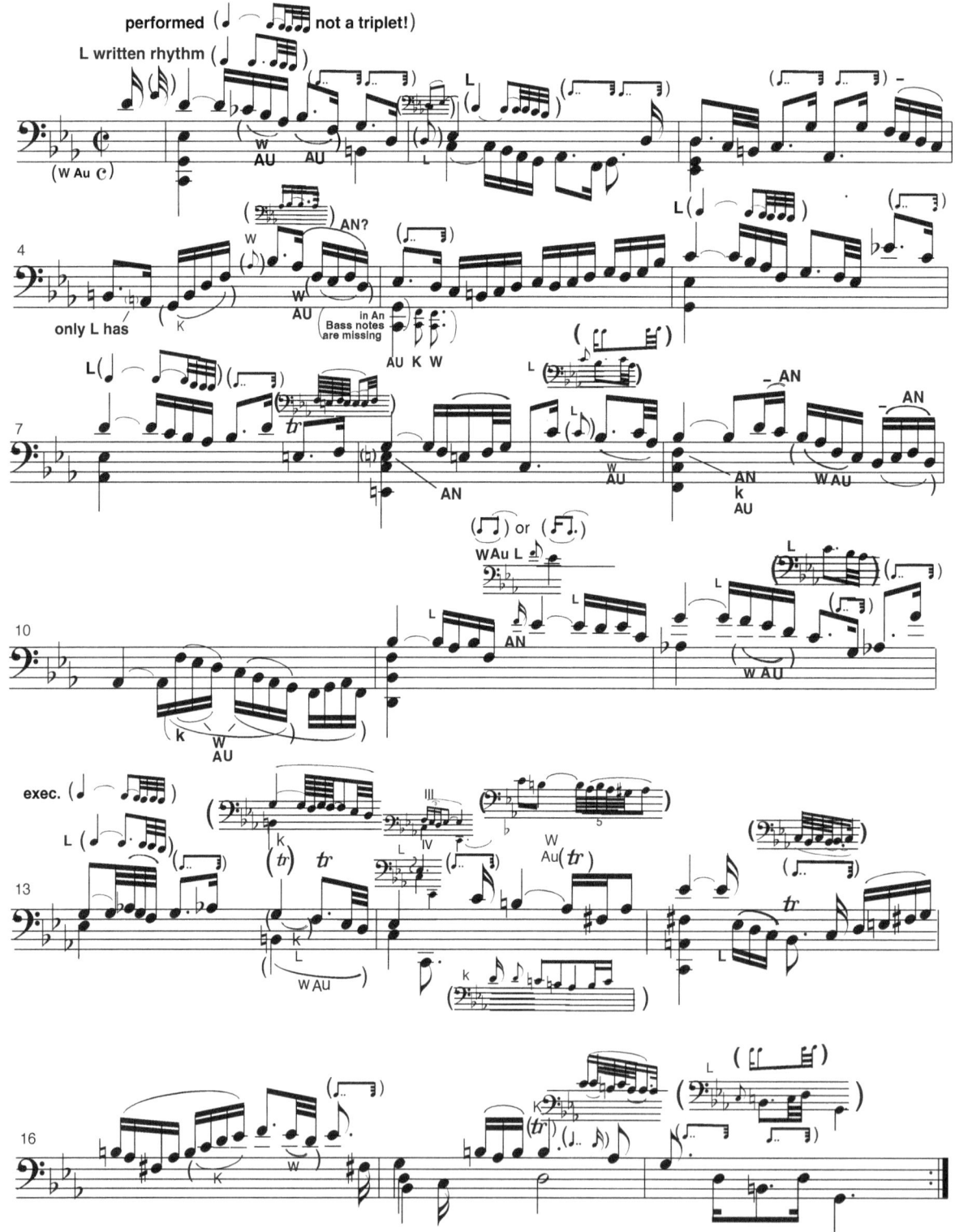

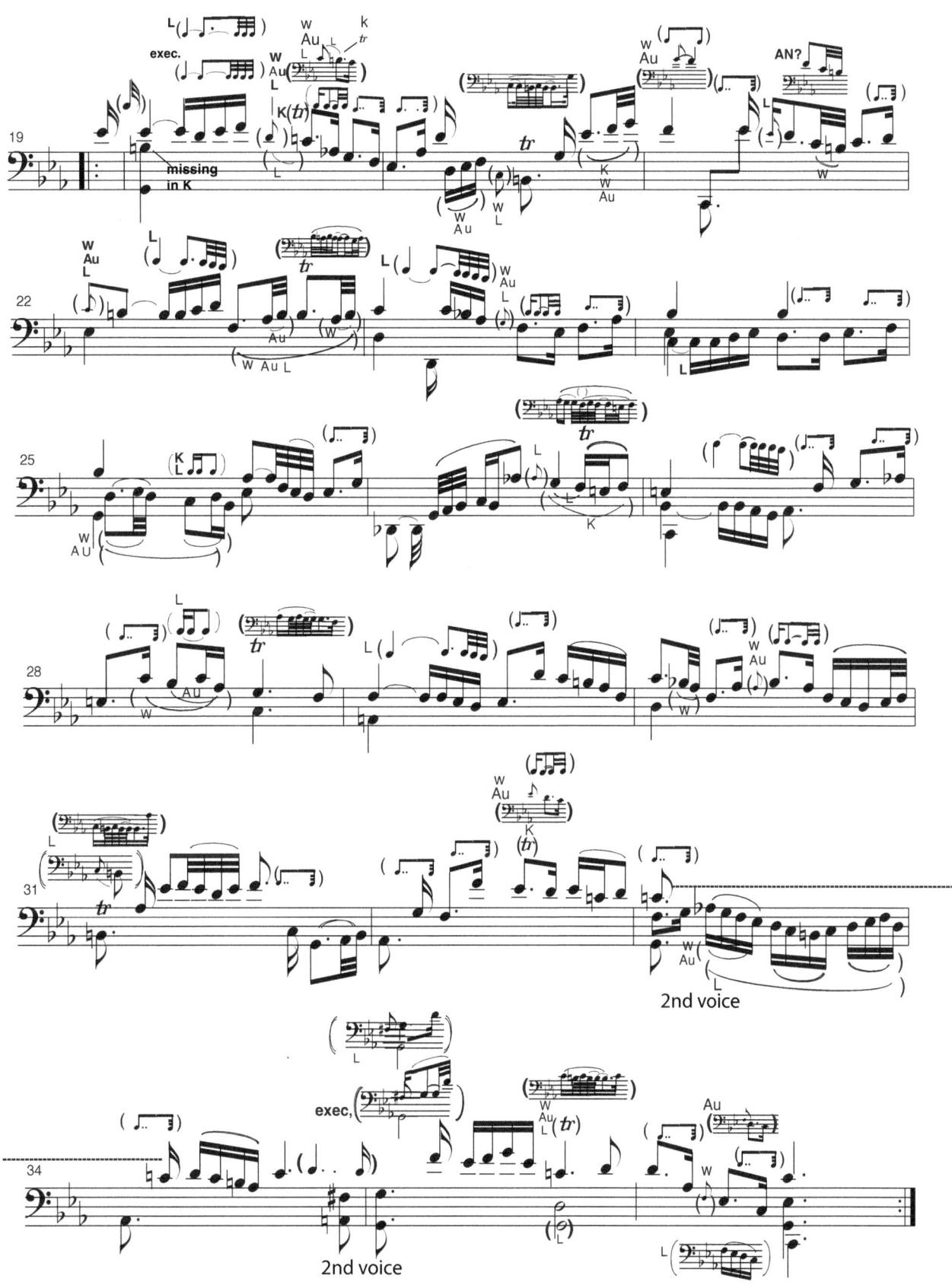

Courante (Scordatura)

This French courante is the only courante in 3/2 in the cello suites. Its basic beat is a relatively heavier ♩
Long notes in the lower voice do not have to be held all their length.

♩. ♪ could be played as ♩.. ♬ (not necessarily all the time)

Uzi Wiesel

The usual meter of a sarabande is  heavy heavier relax Bach strengthened the 2nd beat with a tenser chord or by adding appoggiaturas or *tr* . This sarabande in the lute Ms is written in two staves, the bass voice is on the lower stave. See also the remarks to the sarabande in the normal tuning.

We can speculate that to the simple  Bach added *appoggiatura* thus strenthening the 2nd beat of the meter.

It is advisable to keep the above meter throughout the whole piece even if the phrases in bars 5,6 and 13-15 are different. When absorbing this meter connections and dynamics can be added. The pace of the sarabande is suggested to be a heavier andante in 3 rather than an adagio in 6/8 .

Sarabande
(Scordatura)

The meter

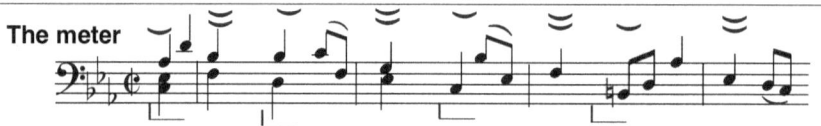

There are many variations of bowings in all the copies and the lute version.
There are also some "slips of the pen" in An and K (An bars 13 and 17, K in bars 7 and 9).

apoggiaturas in W and AU
possible exec. in
the repeat

Gavotte I
(scordatura)

The "building blocks" of this piece are the four beats (mainly triplets), as marked, which are written four times to form a complete sentence (bars 1-4, 4-9, 9-13). Followed are bars 13-15 (only twice the four-beats' group) then a sort of "side remarks" bars 15-16 and 16-17 (two groups of four beats in a form of "questions and answers") followed by two groups of two! beats (bars 17-18) then two groups of six (4+2) bars 18-19 and 20-21 followed by returning to "normal" (bars 21-23) two groups of four beats. All this is masterfully woven.

The meter seems to be

The pace is probably like in gavotte I.

The written ♫♫ if played too fast will sound as if Bach wrote ♫♫ which he didn't.

There are no distinct bowings marks in all the copies and in L. The slurs in all the copies mark only the triplets (except in bars 14-17 in W and AU). One can use slurs over six notes or over three notes (or no slurs!?).

Gavotte II
(scordatura)

Gavotte I da capo

Gigue
(Scordatura)

K's copy has only 9 bars of the gigue.
"There is a pulse beat on each bar" J.J.Quantz
"Gigues must be played extremely fast" Muffat
"Gigue is played with short bow-strokes" Quants

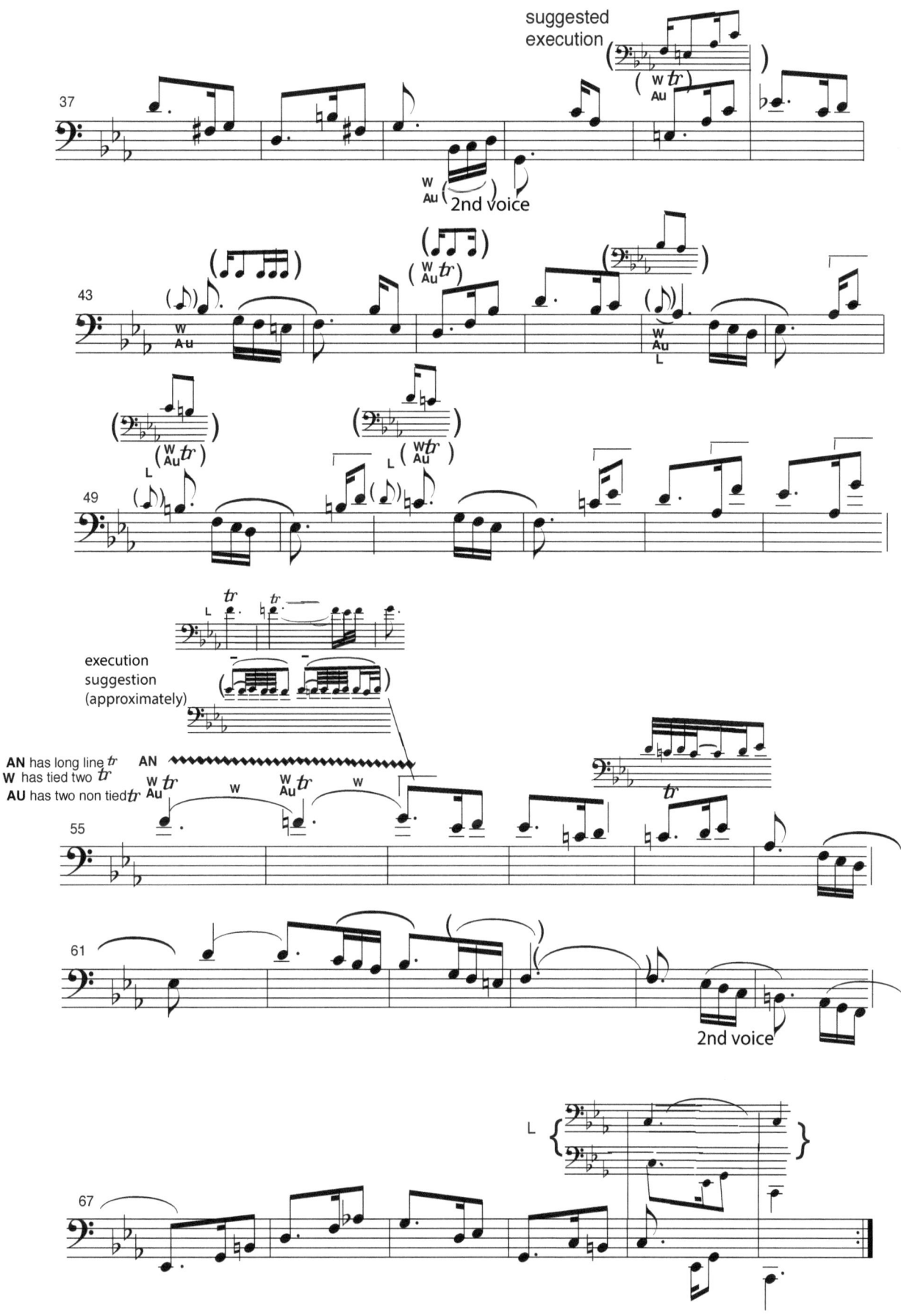

Allemande (performance suggestion) (normal tuning)

Allemande has a cantilena character. This allemande has long lines recitative like.
The copies are not consistant in their bowings. Bowings here are according to AN. Bowings in brackets are from the other copies and L. Bach in L wrote out himself the applications of rhythms in performance (see introduction page 12 example 40). They are marked here in the text. Bowings in the fast passages are optional.

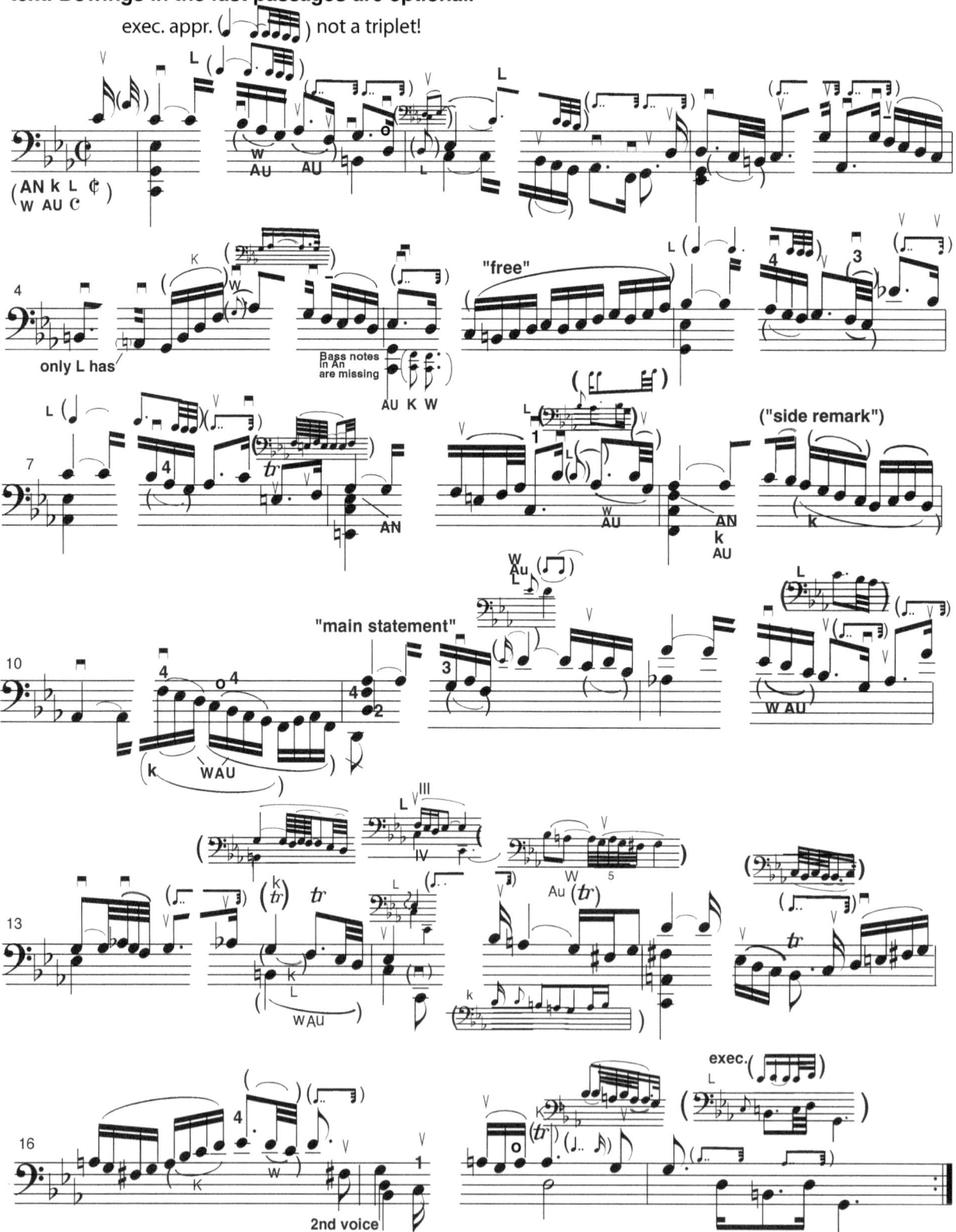

Courante performance suggestion (normal tuning)

This french style courante of the 5th suite is in 3/2. Its basic beat is a heavier 𝅗𝅥.
Long bass notes do not have to be held all their length.

♩. ♪ could be played as ♩.. ♬

Sarabande 5th suite remarks

This wonderful sarabande, more than any other movement from the solo suites by J.S.Bach, is often played as a separate piece of music. It is performed on many solemn occasions and as an encore.
Players are sometimes carried away and play the sarabande as a personal self-expressive movement in slow 6 beats! like:

A sarabande in its nature is in 3 beats with the meter of heavy-heavier-relax.
The 2nd beat is stressed by Bach with tenser harmonic chords or by appoggiaturas:

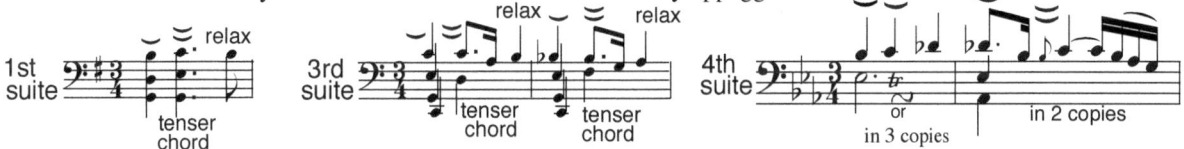

Bach uses often the form of the sarabande. Here are 2 examples:
The Goldberg Variations for cembalo. In the theme we notice the stressed heaviness of the 2nd beat.
 If this meter is kept throughout all the variations the work will have a special aura. Also one notices the structure of a two-bars unit, as marked, while keeping the individual bars' meter:

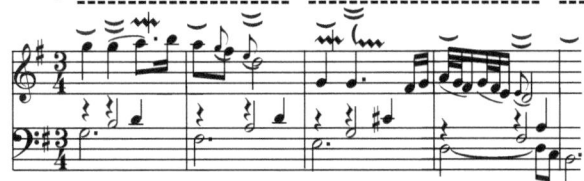

A similar example is the chaccone (Bach's title "ciaccona") from the 2nd partita for violin solo:

We can find here the same meter of a sarabande as if starting on the 1st beat of the 1st bar!
Keeping the sarabande meter throughout the whole chaccone will create a special consistant mood..

The sarabande of the 5th suite has the same features. Yet it has something unique which is often overlooked.
Here is its basic "simple" line:

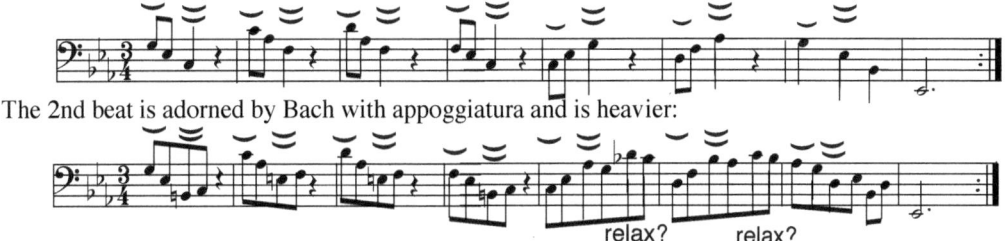

The 2nd beat is adorned by Bach with appoggiatura and is heavier:

The MS of the lute version of the 5th suite is written in 2 staves! The relaxed 3rd beat is like another "voice":

Lute version (transposed)

So here are the 2 "voices" in one stave:

The usual meter of a sarabande is $\frac{3}{4}$ heavy heavier relax

Bach strengthens the 2nd beat with a tenser chord or by adding appoggiaturas or tr. This sarabande in the lute ms is written in two staves, the bass voice is on the lower stave.

It is advisable to keep the above meter throughout the whole piece even if the phrases in bars 5,6 and 13-15 are different. On the basis of this meter, connections and dynamics can be added. The pace of the sarabande is a heavier andante in 3 rather than an adagio in $\frac{6}{8}$ (see "sarabande remarks" the preceeding page).

Sarabande (normal tuning)

One meter-unit has a group of four beats. The 1st beat is strogly articulated while the 3rd beat (the barline) is stressed "a pulse beat falls on each bar" Quantz. " It is advisable not to play the 4th beat of a meter-unit as an intentional dynamic upbeat in order not to disturb the meter which is the natural breathing of the organism.

Gavotte I performance suggestion (normal tuning)

The "building blocks" of this piece are the 4 beats (as marked down) which are written 4 times to form a complete sentence. Followed (from the repeat sign) are twice the 4 beats' groups then 1 group of 4 beats and extra "side remarks" of groups of 2 beats and ending with 5 groups of 4 beats! All this is masrerfully woven.

The pace resembles gavotte I. The meter like in gavotte I is a unit of 4 beats, where the 1st is articulated and the 3rd is stressed (barlines) "there is a pulse beat on each bar" J.J.Quantz

The meter

The written  ♪♪♪ ♪♪♪ if played too fast will sound as if Bach wrote ♪♪♪ ♪♪♪ which is not the case (also faster virtuosity is lacking charm).

There are no bowings in this Gavotte in the four copies and the Lute version except in bars 15-18 (the slurs in the 1st bar are for the triplets!). One can use slurs over groups of three notes or over six notes or no slurs at all

Gavotte II performance suggestion normal tuning

Gavotte I da capo

Gigue performance suggestion (normal tuning)

K's copy has only 9 bars of the gigue.
"There is a pulse beat on each bar" J.J.Quantz

Bach recreated few of his works for different instruments (from cembalo to violin and vice versa or i.e.the prelude in e major for violin solo rewritten for a full orchestra as an overture to a cantata). This recreation of the 5h suite's lute version for cello illuminates Bach's rich harmonies which are often a sort of "guessing" in the other suites also it is a panorama of Bach several "voices" writing in one stave. There are no added personal notes in this recreation to Bach's own text.

The adaptation is transposed from g minor to c minor. The player can be flexible in the chord playing i.e. the lower bass notes could sometimes be played separately, or one can roll the chord and stay longer on the upper voice. Long bass notes, in the double-stops don't have to be held all their length.

The present version should be played flowingly and naturally with long statements regardless of some "difficulties" with the double-stops.

In the slower opening there is a 𝆏 pulse and "heavy" ♩ beats . This helps the choice of tempo.

In the lute Ms there are fewer bowings owing probably to the plucking nature of playing the instrument. It seems that the written ties (legato) directions, are for defining musical ideas and contrasts and not technical execution directions (sometimes they may be for both purposes). Most of the bowing suggestions in this version are taken from the 4 copies and there are some personal additions.

Prelude normal tuning after Lute MS

ALLEMANDE normal tuning after Lute Ms

In the lute version Bach himself wrote the rhythmic applications of the written text in performance. The use of these applications was always flexible, never dogmatic or automatic. Bach uses them in bars 1, 2, 6, 7, 13, 19, 22, 23, 25, 27, and 29 but not in bars 11, 12 and 24. L has very few bowings directions so most of the suggestions are from the 4 copies

(2nd voice)

Courante normal tuning after Lute Ms.

This french style courante is the only one in the cello suites in 3/2. Its basic pulse is ♩ with a "heavier" beat of 𝅗𝅥.
Long notes in the lower voice do not have to be held all their length.

The usual meter of the *saranbande* is heavy heavier relax

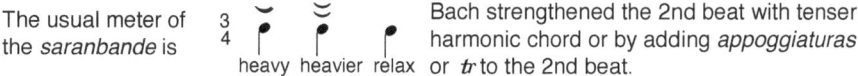

Bach strengthened the 2nd beat with tenser harmonic chord or by adding *appoggiaturas* or *tr* to the 2nd beat.

This sarabande i written in the lute MS in two staves. It is advisable to hold its basic meter throughout the piece and keep a heavier andante in 3 rather than an adagio in 6/8.

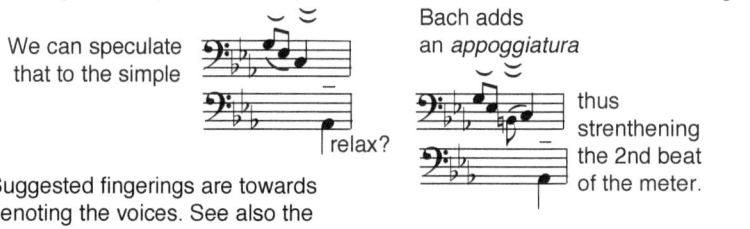

We can speculate that to the simple

Bach adds an *appoggiatura*

thus strenthening the 2nd beat of the meter.

Suggested fingerings are towards denoting the voices. See also the special remarks in the performance suggestion version.

Sarabande after Lute Ms. (normal tuning)

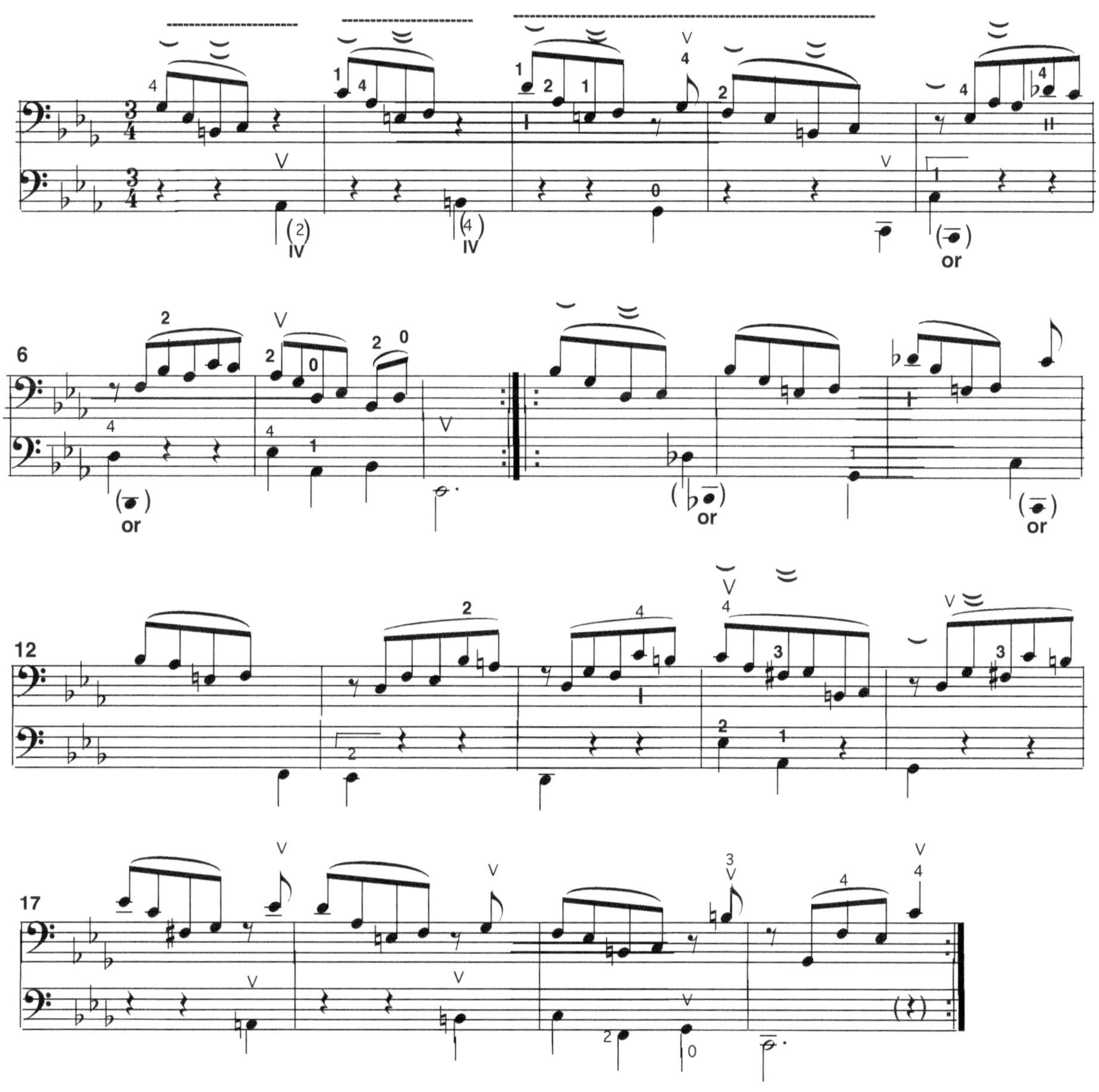

Gavotte I
normal tuning after Lute Ms.

One meter-unit has a group of four notes. The 1st beat is articulated while the 3rd beat (the barline) is stressed "a pulse beat falls on each bar" Quantz."
It is advisable not to play the 4th beat of a meter-unit as an intentional dynamic upbeat in order not to disturb the meter, the natural breathing of the organism..

There are almost no bowings in this Gavotte in the four copies and the Lute version except in bars 15-18 (all the written slurs are for the triplets!). One can use slurs over groups of three notes or over six notes (or no slurs at all).
The meter like in gavotte I is a unit of four beats, the 1st is articulated and the 3rd is stressed (bar lines).

In execution, in order to bring out the main voice, a use of a light bow and shorter (in time) bass notes is suggested throughout the basses.

Gavotte I da capo

Gigue normal tuning after Lute Ms.

"The Gigue is played with short and light bow strokes" (Quantz)
"Gigues must be played extremely fast" (Muffat 1653-1704)
"...A pulse beat on each bar" (Quantz)

Suite VI

BMV 1012

PRELUDE
ALLEMANDE
COURANTE
SARABANDE
GAVOTTE I - GAVOTTE II
GIGUE

Bach wrote the 6th Suite for an instrument with 5 strings (an added upper e string) thus enlarging the range of playable notes.

Playing the suite on the four strings cello may pose some difficulties for players, but performance should be in the same flowing manner and expression as in the other suites.

The bowings in all the copies are inconsistent. AN has some dynamics in the Prelude, W and AU add more.

The editor's remarks, the choice of non-binding bowings (based mainly on AN) and the suggested fingerings, try to help form a concept towards a meaningful rendering, and a richer architectonic texture with voices, shades, lines and meter.

Suite 6 prelude performance remarks

I) Articulation: In the first 2 bars' exposition, and the equivalents later on, a subtle bow articulation is needed
the essence of the music is

The articulation suggestion is that in each of the 3 notes' groups more bow could be used on the marked notes (1st and 3rd) to clarify the "voices", the same from the 3rd bar, less bow for the 2nd voice

likewise in similar passages:

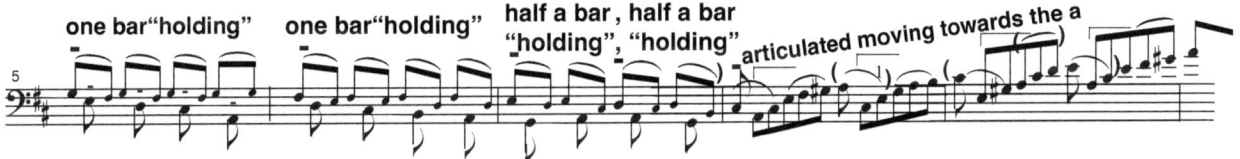

II) Musical energy: Musical energy is sometimes a *sostenuto* type, steady "holding" rhythmically, while in other passages musical energy moves constantly towards a point of arrival

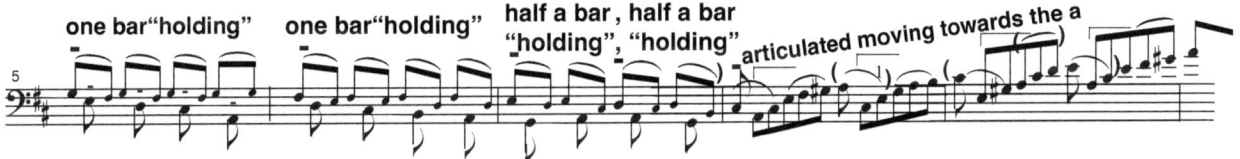

Likewise "moving" down towards the e

III) Architectonic conception: Bach introduces his main idea, the exposition, in bars 1-7 then the transition bars 8-11 to the 2nd exposition in a . The energy builds up gradually to the climax in bar 74. From there on, to the end, everything slowly abates in intensity where to bar 100 where in returning to d calm is restored, one may think that after all the happenings there is "peace with God".

Bowings mainly according to AN with added variations from the other copies. The smaller typed notes indicate the relatively "less important" ones. Bowings suggestions help articulate the rhetorics.

Prelude PERFORMANCE SUGGESTION

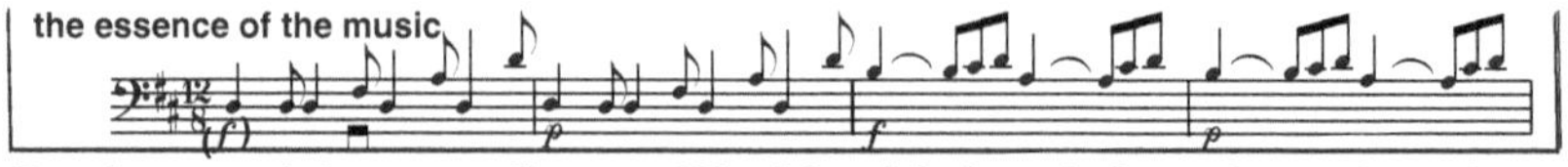

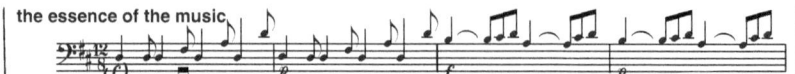

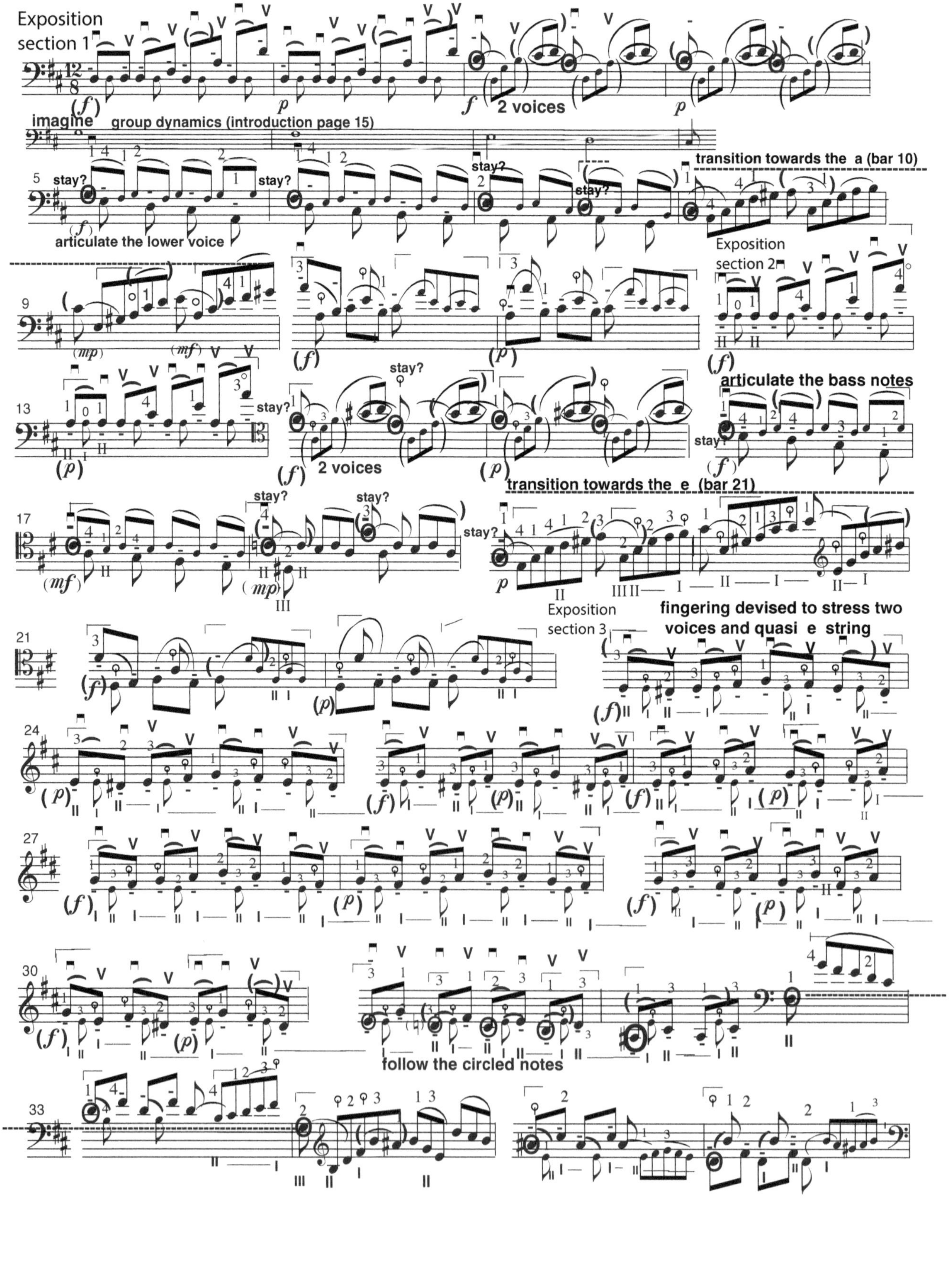

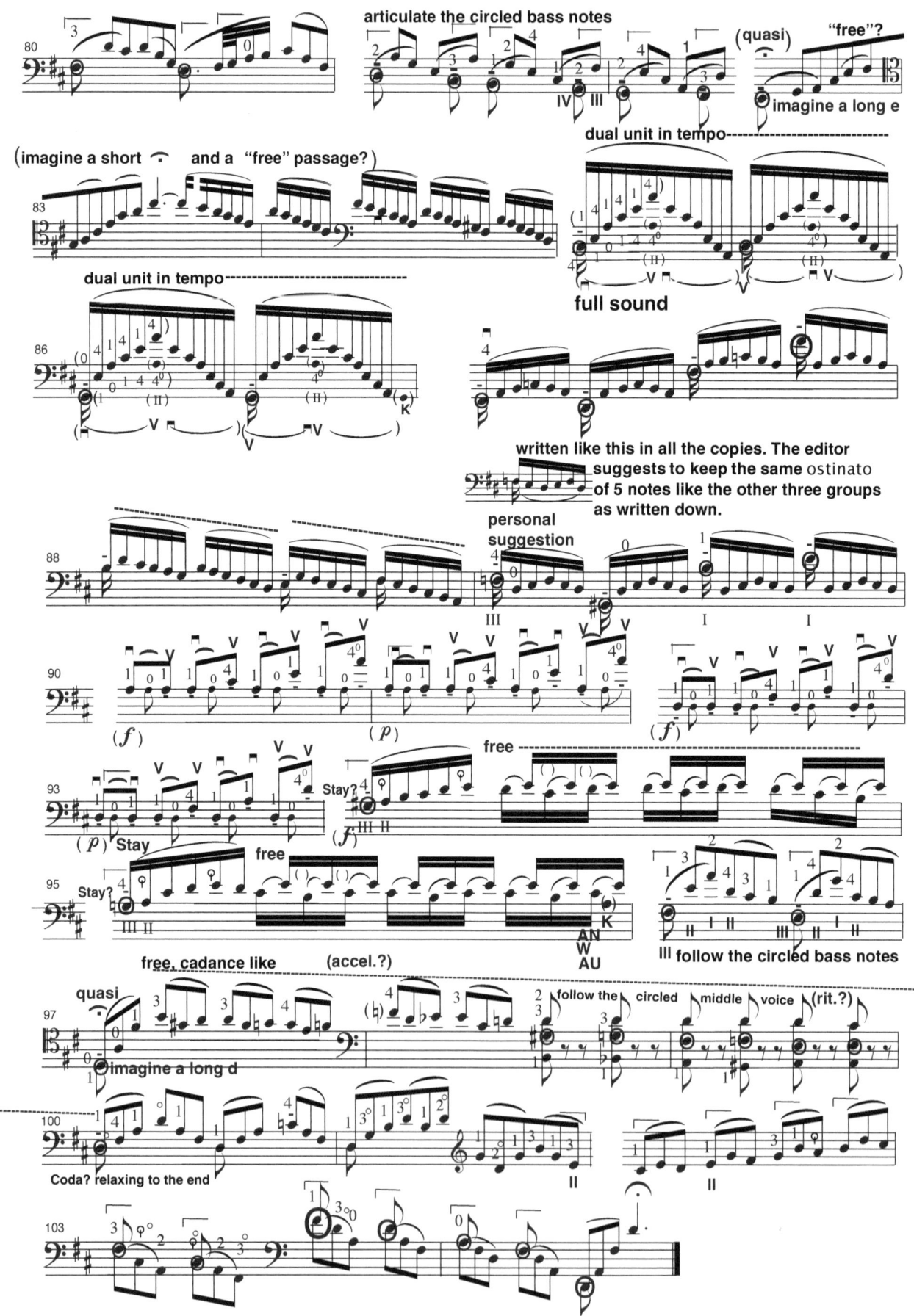

Suite 6 allemande performance remarks

I) Tempo: To the title allemande K added Adagio, W and AU added molto Adagio. This allemande is a special recitative-like slow movement where Bach employs ♪ and ♬ rythmical values.

In the long ornamental musical lines the single notes are not individully very important. The Adagio or molto Adagio are to be interpreted as slow or very slow as long as the whole lines are there in the consciousness of the player and as long as the listner is conscious of them.
The player with taste is free with flexible speed between the start and the end of lines. The complete lines of the phrases help us to choose a tempo

II) Triplets: The writing of the dotted rhythms in Bach's works has to be understood correctlly

written ♩. ♬ was applied and played approximately ♩~♬

written ♩. ♬ was applied and played approximately ♩.~♬

Triplets always have a tie sign or number 3 above them

2 examples where Bach imself applied these rhythms

"French overture" for the cembalo (1733). In the later version (1735) he put the actual rhythms to be played :

allemande suite 5

In the following 2 examples from the cello suites the editors of the Baerenreiter esteemed critical performed edition made the regrettable mistake of misintepreting Bach's rythmical writing and put triplets (regardless the fact that whenever there is a triplet there is ⌢3 over it

Here are the 2 examples

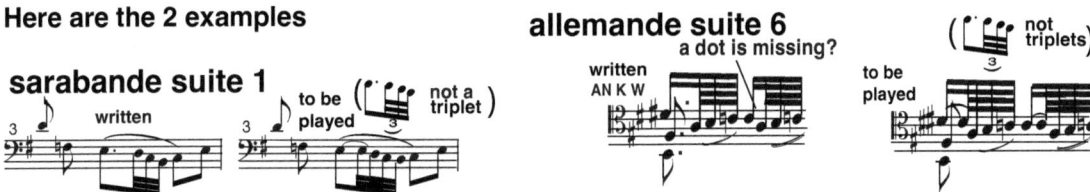

K added **Adagio**
W and Au added **molto Adagio.**

Bowings according to AN (bowings and embellishments in brackets are from other copies).
The applications of the non written double dotted rhythms are marked in the text. The long bass notes do no have to be held for their whole length. Fingerings try to help the rhetorics.
The *recitative* like character of this allemande calls for an imaginative freedom of expression within the meter and the architectonic form.

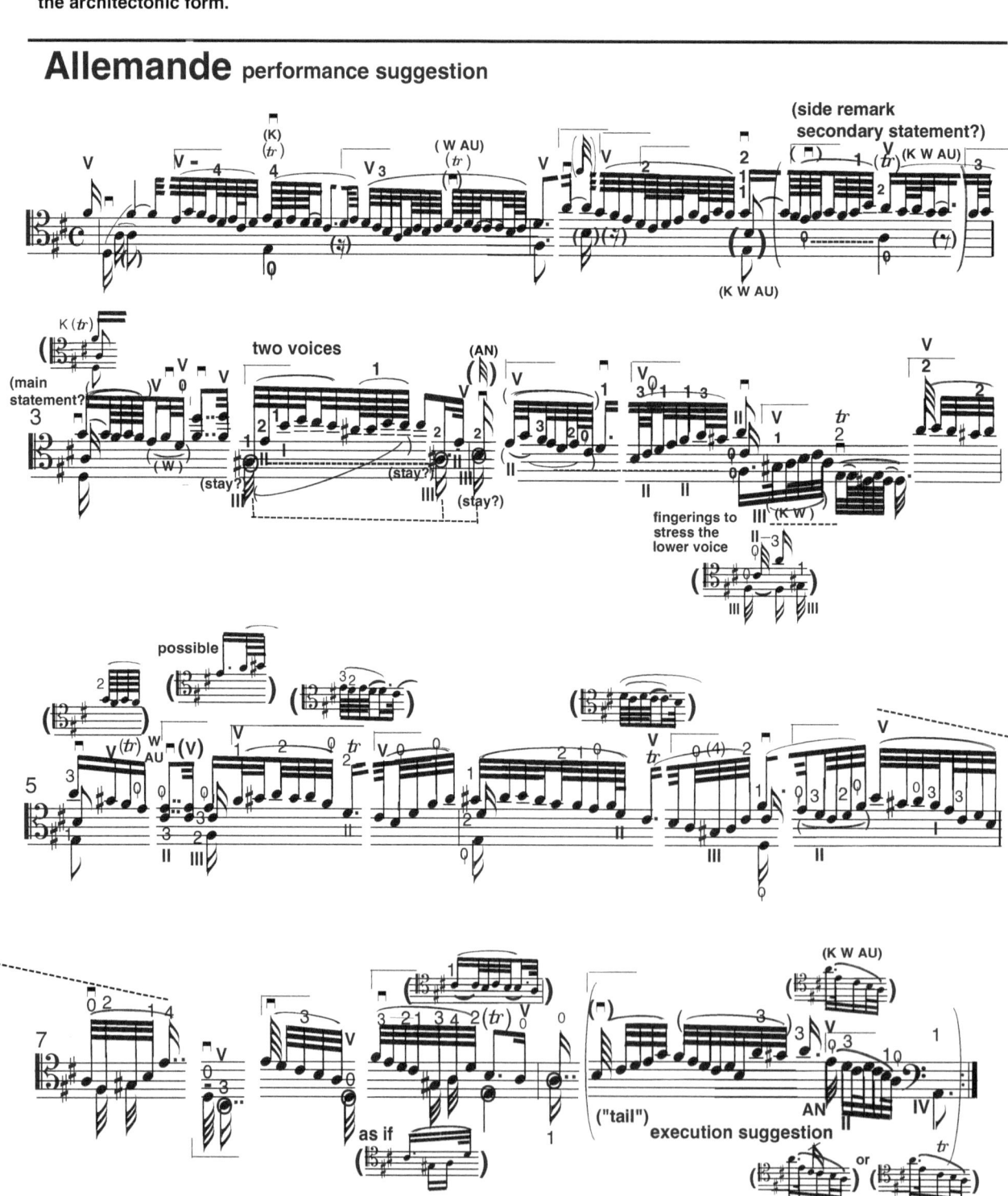

Allemande performance suggestion

This courante is a moderately-fast Italian type corrente in 3/4 like the ones in the 1st, 3rd and 4th suites. It is different from the french type in the 5th suite in 3/2. The bowings in this courante in all the copies including AN, are not consistant in their markings. In the following text the bowings are based on AN (above the notes), with some suggestions in brackets from the other copies (marked under the notes) also some editor's suggestions. The syntax division is marked by ----------
The meter changes all the time ("...in order to arouse" K.P.E.Bach).

COURANTE performance suggestion

different versions in the copies for 1st beat of 31

The dotted lines show the gavotte's meter (four rapid ♩ notes). The 4th beat of the meter-unit of 4 (marked in brackes) should be treated as an end part of the unit.
In addition "a pulse beat falls on each bar".
Bowings according to AN are above the notes. Bowings from other copies are in brackets under the stave.

GAVOTTE I performance suggestion

GAVOTTE II performnce suggestion
"solo trio" as a contrast to gavotte 1 ("tutti").

gavotte I Da Capo

"Gigues must be played extremely fast" (Muffat 1735?). "... it is played with short light bow-strokes" ..."a pulse beat falls on each bar" (Quantz 1751).

The gigue is based on the "building stone" of 2 bars. Important is the articulation of the 2 voices. The bowings in AN are not clear enough and need editing (also in the other copies).

Gigue performance suggestion

Uzi Wiesel has been playing and teaching the J.S. Bach Cello Suites for most of his life.

He is a winner of several international prizes including the Piatigorski Prize (USA 1953), International Concours (Moscow 1953) and the Pablo Casals International Concours (1961). The Israel Council for Culture and Arts awarded him a special national prize (1975). In November 1996 he was honoured by Indiana University USA with the title "Chevalier du Violoncelle", "in recognition of his universal contributions to the art of playing and teaching the cello". In April 2007 Uzi Wiesel received the Government of Israel coveted prize for life achievement.

After his graduation with honours from the Juilliard School of Music in New York (1954) he spent some time with Pablo Casals in Prades, France.

Among a vast repertoire he dedicates much time to Baroque music as well as 20th century repertoire including performances of the concerti by Luciano Berio (Milano, Berio conducting), Ligeti (ICSM), and Lutoslawski (Copenhagen, EBU direct broadcast to all Europe). A dedicated supporter of Israeli music, he has premiered and recorded many concerti and solo pieces written and dedicated to him by Israeli composers.

Uzi Wiesel has performed with artists such as Menuhin, Barenboim, Zuckerman, Perlman and Lukas Foss. He was a member and one of the founders of the world renowned Tel Aviv String Quartet.

A dedicated and acclaimed teacher he was a Professor in the Academy of Music in the Tel Aviv University (1965-1996) and guest Professor at the University of New York. Many of his students have won prizes in international competitions and are concertmasters, chamber music players and teachers around the globe. Uzi Wiesel has been a guest teacher in the USA, Germany and Australia, and is frequently invited to give master classes in many countries including the USA, England, Germany, Holland, Russia, and Hungary. For more than 10 years he was chamber music director in the Bayreuth International Youth Festival in Germany, and from 1993 – 2008 he was teaching at the summer academy in Radolfzell.

Uzi Wiesel is often invited to international competitions such as the Rostrpopovich and Feuermann competitions as a jury member. He took part in the International Cello Congresses in Washington as a performer and panel member.

His articles has been published in The "Strad" magazine.

www.ingramcontent.com/pod-product-compliance
Lightning Source LLC
Chambersburg PA
CBHW042138290426
44110CB00002B/47